"To the singers of the future who aspire to greatness, I recommend this book. To those singers of today who wish to learn the secret, this...
- JOHN ROBERTSON, Director of Cameron Mackintosh Australia

CAN ANYBODY SING?

GETTING THE BEST OUT OF THE VOICE YOU HAVE

AMANDA COLLIVER

"Amanda is a truly unique singing practitioner, and this book reflects the kaleidoscopic colours of her teaching. In vivid detail she manages to portray the complex relationship between singing technique and artistry. This book is a welcome addition to the singing world".
CHRIS NOLAN - Singer, composer, Arranger, Musical Director - Mountview Academy of Theatre Arts, London

"Amanda Colliver is a name that has been linked with the stars of all the major commercial productions in Australia, and it is without a doubt that her tuition and professional guidance have played a huge part in my being cast in this role."
CHLOE DALLIMORE (Ulla - The Producers)

"Amanda works with the kind of knowledge and empathy that can only be borne from extensive personal experience. There was no doubt in my mind to whom I would entrust the voices of Nicole Kidman and Ewan McGregor in Baz Lurhmann's Moulin Rouge."
ANDREW ROSS, Musical Director, Arranger, Musician

"Amanda understands that great work in acting, dancing, and singing not only come from the command of technique, but also from the emotional impulses deep inside the artist. Her book is a guide to finding those inner impulses and is laced with sound advice."
ELLIS JONES - Head of Acting, Royal Academy of Dramatic Art, London

"Amanda approaches every student on his or her own merit hand in hand with unfailing consideration, support, and interest. Her reputation goes before her in the Performing Arts community. She is as good as it gets."
SHAUN MURPHY - Performer, Director, Composer

"Rather than being a how-to-do book, Can Anybody Sing? offers the reader a gateway to the place where singing and life are united."
DR. JOHN SHARPLEY - Composer, Co-founder Opera Viva Singapore

"Amanda is a woman of passion and positive energy. Her devotion and dedication to her work is evident in every chapter of this wonderful book. Read it and you will benefit beyond your expectations!"
VIKAS MALKANI - Founder - SoulCentre, Asia's Premier Centre for Personal Development

"I have long been intrigued by Amanda's teaching approach after hearing many glowing testimonies from her students and witnessing many a stunning vocal outcome after her care. This book gives us great insight into the secrets of her success and provides an invaluable tool to all singers on their journey towards vocal and self-discovery. I highly recommend it to singers of all genres, including the shower-singer."
DEBBIE PHYLAND - Speech Pathologist & Voice Consultant

"Sam Worthington (star of Avatar) was just one of the students to be profoundly influenced by Amanda's teaching."
TONY KNIGHT - Head of Acting, NIDA

"Amanda helps her students explore a vocal production that is natural and instinctive, by offering them choices to meet their individual needs and job demands. Her careful, constructive, and suggestive comments, along with a friendly, fun atmosphere, allow an environment of confidence and safety."
TANEE POONSUWAN - Voice coach, Scenario Theatre Company, Bangkok

"Amanda has synthesised her training and experience to develop an excellent technical approach to singing. Her lateral approach allows her to adjust her methods to suit the needs of every individual."
VANESSA FALLON ROHANNA - ASDA, BMus (Voice) NSW Conservatorium of Music, Post Grad Dip.

Can Anybody Sing?

Getting The Best Out Of The Voice You Have

AMANDA COLLIVER

PaperKite Studios

Can Anybody Sing?

Getting The Best Out Of The Voice You Have

by AMANDA COLLIVER

© 2012 PaperKite Studios. All rights reserved.

ISBN 978-1-4836-3768-6 (Paperback)

ISBN 978-1-4836-3769-3 (EPub)

Special thanks to:

SoulCentre founder and mentor Vikas Malkani for his generous permission to utilise selected material from his Life Coaching courses *Shine, Evolve* and *Bloom*

Life coaching principle - *Be, Do, Have* –The Rainbow Gathering, pg 27-28

IP Diagram *The Fear Factor* - You and Me Against the World, pg 76 & 77

Story of the frog in the saucepan - Rhythm and Ritual, pg 91

Story of the two boys at the ocean's edge - The Head to the Heart (*Power section*), pg 99

FOREWORD

Searching for words to describe Amanda Colliver was more difficult than I had expected. Not the sort of difficult where I needed a Thesaurus or Lexicon or Dramaturg, but just because there's so much of her to describe.

Firstly, there is the person who takes so much delight in her own mortality, which alone is overwhelming.

Secondly, her skills as a singer, composer, and lyricist are astonishing and have the capacity to touch one in a deep, deep place.

Thirdly, she understands the human condition which - in my book - tells me she's got it taped!

And lastly, she knows pain and joy and all that lies in between. She intuitively knows who you are, what you have, and most importantly what you need, and it is this that, in all its complexity and mystery, she taps into so expertly, so clearly and honestly, without agenda.

This book is timely.

It is for now.

It is for us.

It is a sharing from one who really, really cares.

Michael Corbidge
Actor, author, playwright,
Senior Voice and Text Coach
The Royal Shakespeare Company

In loving memory of

RJ Rosales and Emma Yong

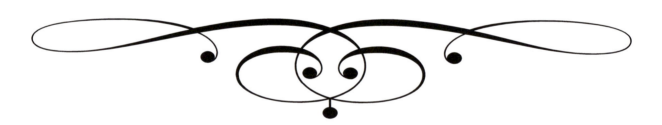

DEDICATED *to all my students - past, present, and future. Thank you for your courage, your gifts, and your journey, but most of all...for allowing me to lead the way.*

and

Dinesh Senan*, without whose dogged belief in building a legacy and sharing one's light with the world, this book would never have been written.*

Notes from the Author

I'm not sure what it was that prompted me to take the enormous leap from my idyllic surroundings on the east coast of Sydney to the relentless commercialism and heat of Singapore other than an intuitive knowing that, in the midst of a successful career and a booming teaching practice, something was missing and I was in danger of settling into a proverbial fur-lined rut. I have always said that I fear stagnation more than change but, as with many of my wise proclamations, I had never placed myself in a situation that showed me what deep change really meant. Leaving my country, family, and friends quickly removed any opportunity I had to rely on past glories or co-dependent relationships and I suddenly found myself drowning in the unresolved dregs of my life.

Some wonderful new friendships and the familiar demands of teaching helped to keep my head above water until a light at the end of the longest tunnel finally beckoned me towards a new beginning and a very different future. This new beginning, however, contained a very pointed message telling me that the left part of my brain was sadly underdeveloped and, if unaddressed, would prevent me from progressing any further in my career and in my life. Unwelcome help came in the form of templates, formulas, mind maps, and strategic business plans, taking every ounce of energy I had to remain open, interested, and the least bit receptive. On the other hand, being someone who believes that we are all co-creators in our own reality, I was able to see that the very things I was resisting were, in essence, exactly what I had to embrace to set me free from my past and usher me into a new paradigm.

Performers who are in control of their own creative work are a minority, and there seems to be very little in the way of palatable information on running one's own business that remotely accommodates the right brain sensibilities of an artist. However, without some kind of strategic planning to actualise one's creative endeavors, many of us continue to put our lives in the hands of partners, corporations, managers, and agents without exploring how much work we can actually generate and control ourselves.

In 2011 a profound and life-changing reading from a Chinese astrologer shone a glaring light on the fact that my successful career both as a teacher and a performer had been based on little more than my ability to be a stunning *cog* in someone else's wheel. It appeared that my own creative fire was barely alight but in that moment of realisation, I felt a palpable shift in my understanding of what the true purpose and direction of my life should and would be. The pursuit of fame and fortune had always felt vacuous and illusory to me and yet the shining beacon of leadership and learning has always beckoned, waiting patiently for the underdeveloped parts of myself to catch up with the one who is ready to forge ahead into the uncharted territory of total trust and commitment to my own potential and power. Birthing this book has been a time of immense joy and satisfaction, carrying me through some of the most difficult moments of my life. Understanding and accepting that there is no real lasting or reliable safety in the external world has reminded me of the importance of interdependent relationships and the need to nurture and develop one's own resourcefulness and creativity. Leading others to this place is where I will eventually contribute and offer the most.

Never has there been such a time of isolation and desperation in the world, where so many do not know where to turn for solace and care. Therefore, never has it been more important for us to seek out what it is we truly believe and to begin taking personal responsibility for our dreams, aspirations, and emotional healing. Joy, celebration, and creative expression are our God-given right but fear, judgement, and the endlessly perpetuated belief that we are *not good enough* make the very things intrinsic to our nature an illusive speck on an unreachable horizon. This can never change unless we are willing to stand empty and unsure while we let go of the things that no longer serve us and reclaim all that we have given up in the name of conformity. Being who we are does not imbue violence or anarchy, but rather a revolutionary shift within that nurtures wisdom and change via the gentle channels of empathy, compassion, and love.

There is no real destination to arrive at in life, just a series of *train stations* along the way to who knows where. The best of plans will undoubtedly go awry and those we thought would be there, by our side, forever, will only travel part of the distance with us. But just as the sun appears to be setting on sorrow and despair, someone else climbs aboard and a wonderful new adventure begins.

My only wish for all of you who read this book is that on this particular train ride you will be reminded of the things you have forgotten about yourself: your power, your potential, your beauty, and your inherent worthiness, but most importantly, that you are not alone.

Welcome aboard!
With love,

Amanda

Contents

Foreword	i
Notes From The Author	iv
Introduction	1
Nature And Nurture	4
Life's A Pitch	10
Breathing	16
The Rainbow Gathering	24
The X Factor	30
The Crocodile Pit	36
Build On The Rock	42
The Grand Canyon	46
Lost In Translation	54
Child's Play	60
Everybody Says, "Dont!"	66
You And Me Against The World	72
My, Myself And I	82
Rhythm And Ritual	90
The Head To The Heart	98
Conclusion	104
Acknowledgements	105

INTRODUCTION

"Amanda, you really must write a book!" This was not the first time I had heard these words and although I had, in fact, thought about documenting my work for several years, the truth was I had no clue how I would rise to the challenge of translating the information I carried in my head into clear, concise sentences on a page. The foundation of my teaching methodology came not only from extensive technical knowledge and performing experience gathered over three decades as a professional opera singer, but also from a place of deep, intuitive knowing. My voracious interest in all things *unseen*, and several hundred student case studies, had left no doubt in my mind that the psychological state of a singer was at the root of all vocal difficulty and that the physical manifestations of it were merely a symptom. I was more than daunted at the prospect of describing the many different approaches I might use when working with different people, and unsure if I could meet the complex demands of explaining why it is that although most singers are generally alike, no two people perceive things in exactly the same way. On the other hand, I was tired of working with disempowered artists who had either undertaken years of training without improvement or were giving up their creative aspirations due to the ignorant cliché "You either have it or you don't." I was becoming increasingly frustrated with the introduction of confusing terminology, half-baked methodologies, elitist attitudes about musical genres, and fearful thinking about vocal damage. Ageist views, intolerance for the natural vocal process, and the ineffectual results of medication prescribed to those suffering from the debilitating effects of performance anxiety left me dismayed and angry. But, suddenly, I was feeling excited at the prospect of offering constructive solutions to the problems I was seeing singers facing both in their training and in their careers, and as one of my business colleagues once said to me, it would be remiss of me not to.

Not all change can be called progress, as many trends of the 21st century are responsible for hindering individual creativity and self-expression. Although these trends enjoy their own particular brand of *colour and movement*, the complex layers of the *human instrument* cannot be treated as a disposable commodity or be expected to enjoy any kind of integrity or longevity. It's interesting to watch the change in vocal mentality as reality shows like *American Idol*, *X Factor* and *The Voice* begin to take over as primary authorities on what is considered to be good singing. For obvious reasons of program formatting, time constraints, and the perverse delight viewers get from seeing a celebrity panel deconstruct and demoralise performers, these shows have no ability or interest in helping wannabe singers understand the ins and outs of vocal technique. Admittedly they have their place and their mass appeal but, as a teacher, I'm seeing a generic vocal mindset in students based on the misleading information common to so many of these shows. The belief that success is guaranteed if you can sing multiple high notes loudly and repetitively, whether or not it's relevant to the style of the song, and nail the climax in 16 bars is an illusory pre-requisite to fame and fortune. This misconception is not only creating a climate of meaningless over-singing but also contributing to a significant rise in vocal damage. The operatic arena remains largely unscathed due to the sheer technical demand and non-negotiable discipline of the style, but the consistency with which renowned opera singers are sharing the stage with rock stars suggests that this genre is also in danger of becoming a casualty of the current industry mindset. An ever-growing emphasis on age, size, and shape gives the impression that those who do not fit the stereotypical requirements are not eligible for the same benefits as those who do. This is particularly true for the younger generation, which has no experience in the broader attitudes of previous times and is now growing up in what I believe to be a vocally unsupportive environment. However, that being said, if something is innate, organic and reliable in its function, which singing is, it doesn't matter how we cover or compromise it; these principles will always be there. Global perceptions may have changed, but the muscular co-ordinations that result in sound have not. Therefore, despite superficial realities and the promise of overnight stardom, anyone serious about developing as a singer will intuitively know that the answers are not found there - and seek to find them somewhere else.

I was an independent child who adored books, trees, music, and animals and gravitated naturally towards all things creative. There was never any doubt that I would choose a life of colour, movement, and song, as I resonated far more deeply with my inner imaginings than the abrasive realities of the external world. By five I was singing at Sunday school, by 12 I was writing poetry and songs, and by 19 I had several years of amateur performing experience behind me and was ready to embark on an operatic career. Teaching singing was never on my agenda, but it literally *found me* when my record producer boyfriend at the time asked me if I would help one of the studio singers with his vocal difficulties. Surprisingly, at twenty-one, I had become a teacher as well as a performer. My upbringing felt strangely contradictory in the way that although my parents were strict and conservative Christians, they were also deeply committed to all things environmental and organic. In hindsight, this combination of religious indoctrination and New Age philosophy planted a perfect seed of discipline and freedom within me. This seed, however, did not grow easily and was stunted for many years by paralysing emotional insecurity that ultimately saw me walk away from performing at the height of my career. The silver lining to this cloud however, was that, through my own personal struggles, I had developed deep empathy with anyone going through the same thing and a passionate desire to help performers reclaim their power and their voices. It is said that "Teachers teach what they most want to learn," which is why this area of my work has been inspiring, rewarding and profoundly healing. To have so many people placing themselves in my care is humbling, but to witness the changes that patience, empathy, and knowledge bring is nothing short of miraculous.

Have you ever wondered where your dreams and aspirations come from, and does it make sense that you would long for the things you have no chance of achieving?

Music is said to be the *universal language* and words are known to have the power of the sword, so if we combine these two elements it appears that the ultimate form of communication is to sing. If the world is a stage and we all stand upon it, this might explain why so many of us have the desire to express ourselves in this way. I used the title *Can Anybody Sing?* not only because it's a frequently asked question, but also because the question is so often misunderstood. Generally, if we're asked if we can do something, we compare ourselves to someone else who is renowned for doing that particular thing well. If we're not as skilled as the person we're comparing ourselves to, the answer is often no. Surely, then, that would mean that if we can't do something as skillfully as an expert, then we have no talent in that area at all. If that were the case, none of us would attempt to do anything, as we can always find someone else more adept at it than we are. The confusion comes when we understand the question to be "Can anybody sing *well?"* which is only relevant when we have established whether or not we all possess the anatomical parts necessary to make sound in the first place. Clearly we do, so we can be confident that it is indeed one of our natural instincts. In essence, the act of singing can appear to be quite simple, but on analysis and execution it reveals itself to be a complex and intricate science. Like any other form of physical expression, true mastery demands discipline, precision, control, and above all, time.

What I love about my work is that there can be no losers in this process, as the experience of singing is our natural, God-given birthright and not limited to a select few. This, of course, does not discount or try to explain how or why there are those born brilliantly aligned and integrated with it or why there are those without any apparent talent at all. This phenomenon, however, should never discourage those of us less aligned with our creative abilities from doing what it takes to access that birthright for ourselves. We all have to start somewhere, so no matter where you are in your vocal development, a passionate desire to learn, a healthy sense of humor, the courage to take action, and the right teacher will most certainly lead to the discovery of your true and authentic voice.

The world is full of *armchair critics* who are, as a friend of mine explained, "those smart enough to understand that there is a problem, but not committed enough to find a solution." That particular conversation struck a profound note in me, and is the primary motivation behind my writing this book. Every day I watch singers overcomplicate the simple things and underestimate the complex, without a clear understanding that there is a perfect but challenging *dance* going on between the body, mind, and spirit which, for many reasons, is out of balance. As we travel these chapters together we will explore the causes of this imbalance, which will point you in the direction of numerous practical and reliable solutions. Exploration of the origins of sound, the human instrument, and breath control will remind you of how much you already have in place when you are born. Explanation and interpretation of confusing terminology, register pitfalls, stylistic versatility and the relevance of classical training for all voices will help you understand negative vocal symptoms and emphasise the importance of becoming open to, and proficient with, musical styles and genres. Chapters on performance anxiety, levels of awareness, educating children, and creating the life you want for yourself will shed light on the psychological barriers to free-flowing sound, the difference between *teaching* and *training* young voices, and the environments conducive to emotional strength and wellbeing. Suggestions for the most effective technical exercises to place and warm up your voice will aid you in the areas of vocal health and maintenance, and a chapter on nature and nurture is geared towards voice educators, emphasising the importance of recognising and catering to the individual needs of every student.

So, dear readers, if you have come this far, you must have a dream to fulfill. And if you continue on until the end of this book, that dream has a greater chance of coming true. It is an honour to have you with me.

1

NATURE AND NURTURE:
Different Strokes for Different Folks

"The measure of a leader is not in how many followers he has, but in how many leaders he creates."

- Abraham Lincoln

There are times in life when we chance upon something that changes the way we view and subsequently approach life, and the previous quote by Abraham Lincoln is one that is never far from my mind or my conversations.

The most charismatic and effective leaders are those who cater to emotional and creative differences in others and, by doing so, encourage the development of independence and strength. To effectively *mentor* another we must know who we are, what we know and what our capabilities are, which is why becoming an educator took me greatly by surprise. Although I was always strong-willed and opinionated, I did not see myself as an innovative thinker or as someone with a burning desire to change things because of my vision of a better way. My only understanding of teaching was of the kind done within the mainstream schooling system, and apart from not having the necessary university qualifications I did not resonate with the dryness of pedagogy and academia. I had, however, always loved to analyse the complexities of the human psyche and had a deep interest in emotional dysfunction and its effect on the body.

I was born number four in a family of five children, which placed seven people beneath one tiny roof. We all had different personalities and each of us needed the individual attention of our parents. This, of course, was not possible as the priority was to feed, clothe, and educate everyone on my father's minimal wage. Wastage of any kind was not tolerated in our home, particularly at meal times. Whether we liked the food or not, everything had to be eaten before we were allowed to leave the dinner table. My elder brother developed a strategy whereby he made sure he misbehaved enough to be sent to his room to eat, and promptly threw the food he hated into the costume chest in the corner of the room. Playing dress ups took on a whole new meaning with several rancid lumps of lambs fry attached to my fairy costume! My particular loathing was for broad beans and runny eggs so whether the food was thrown up or thrown out, wastage appears to have been inevitable.

I gave up on the subject of mathematics when I was eight years old and my class had advanced from the times tables to the complexities of fractions. Trena Crossley was the smartest girl in the class and took to them like a duck to water, but I remember the feeling of rising panic and distress as I fell further and further behind the others. As my teacher did not come back to help me, I assumed that I was probably not very intelligent. In stark contrast Mr Hatzikides, my grade six teacher, would regularly morph into a guitar wielding, wannabe rock star, insisting that we all take time out from our academic studies to explore the world of music and song. Needless to say, I adored him and developed extremely well under his tuition.

In hindsight, I would have thrived in the creative environment of the Rudolph Steiner School, which offers a structured curriculum that is designed to nurture the developmental stages of a child by catering to his or her needs. Steiner's teachings aim to encourage creativity and independent thinking by supporting imagination and freedom of expression in every individual. The resonance I have with this approach contributes to my somewhat unorthodox way of delivering technical information via tangible imagery, anecdotes, and analogies.

Spiritually, I have always been very much at home with the philosophy of Buddhism, which is said to be a way of life rather than a religion. Its fundamental principles focus on personal responsibility, wisdom and integrity and it is my commitment to this way of living that fuels the holistic approach I have of working with students from the *inside out* rather than the *outside in*. The term *holistic* is often perceived to be radical or somewhat 'out there', but it is, in fact, an approach that works not only on the result but also on the parts and layers that contribute to that particular result.

Conversely, the general perception of an opera singer was, and still is, one who is overweight, conservative and old fashioned. So the arrival of someone like me - a thin, bleached hair, leather-clad teenager espousing New Age profundities - was unusual to say the least. I adored the rigor and challenges of operatic technique and moved from chorus member to soloist in a matter of years. But, although I loved this art form, the *gypsy* in me languished and longed for a more contemporary outlet.

Two pivotal personal relationships with musicians introduced me to the world of pop music, songwriting, and studio recording. I met Rudy at a songwriters meeting in Melbourne when I was 19 years old and although he was fifteen years my senior, our connection was immediate. He was an experienced singer, songwriter, musician, composer, recording engineer and arranger, who mentored me in the areas of pop music, songwriting, and studio recording for the next five years. I later met an Irish-Lithuanian *troubadour* called Paul whose extraordinary musical genius served to extend and deepened this knowledge for the better part of seven years. Both of these relationships marked the cornerstone of my ability to cross from one style to another with an understanding and appreciation of the relevance and artistry of them all.

The students I have encountered over the years have been eclectic and extremely varied. Age, race, culture, life experience, and creative preferences have all contributed to the different ways in which each student processes and integrates information. Where one will express fear and trepidation from a lack of performing experience, another will carry so much emotional trauma the body simply will not allow a free sound to emerge. Others will have no difficulty whatsoever embracing new information, integrating it physically, and moving to a higher level of vocal expertise with ease and joy. Although a safe learning environment is essential, it should never become so comfortable that students don't learn to fend for themselves. The responsibility of a teacher is to help you become what you want to become, but he or she cannot *realise* your dreams for you. Subsequently, every singer must learn to become vocally independent. Freedom only comes with choices, and choices must be given and understood before they can be made.

Although I have a very clear understanding of the technical elements I require each singer to master, I see no purpose in their doing what I ask if they do not understand its relevance to the result they are seeking. The action of singing is *automatically suggested* by the body's *understanding* of what the action feels and sounds like, but if there is no actual experience of these sensations, they cannot be imagined, and therefore cannot be created. As with any skill, the action needs to be repeated many times before it becomes an integrated awareness and when it does, the student will reap the benefits of vocal independence.

Insecurity in a student tends to show up in one of two ways: either in defense, or in defenselessness. The students who are fiery and passionate by nature often find it difficult to trust others and therefore rely on defense and judgement as a means of survival. Creatively this can manifest as rigidity and negativity, particularly towards themselves, making them extremely challenging to work with. I have learned that the best approach in this situation is one of consistency and lightness. Consistency on all levels contributes to an environment of safety and trust, and lightness brings balance to the energetic *heaviness* they might be carrying. As the stoic front begins to soften, the immense ability of these individuals begins to shine through. On the other hand, there are those who are constantly looking to someone else for guidance and validation and who are generally lacking in energy and direction. The absence of voiced opinions tends to render them creatively ineffectual, which makes it easy for others to overlook or dominate them. In this situation, I focus the lessons more on strategic thinking and physical empowerment to encourage the student to make his or her own vocal decisions and finally, to execute those decisions with confidence.

I am of the belief that most things in life have been said and done before and that we simply plagiarise and regurgitate information for much of our lives. Therefore, the only thing that makes what we say or do original is the way in which we present it - which carries its own particular genius. I remember a conversation with a colleague during a coffee break at the Australia Opera Company as I was sharing the exciting progress of one of my students. I thought she was joking when she leant over and asked seriously, "You don't reveal all your secrets to them do you?" This person was a very good singing teacher in her own right, but her comment suggested that she not only believed she *owned* the information she was sharing but also that her students might be her *competition* in the future and, therefore, that she needed to be selective about how much of it she gave away. Quite soon after, my judgement of her was to soften when I was forced to face my own daunting *mirror*. The fact that I was a performer as well as a teacher made it inevitable that I would find myself in a situation where I would be competing with a student of mine. Anna and I were asked to audition for the part of 'Claudia' in the Broadway Musical 'Nine', and if I'm honest, I was a little put out that she was auditioning with me in the first place. As Anna sought my reassurance before going in to sing for the panel, the line between performer and teacher suddenly became blurred. I don't remember exactly what I said to her, but I was struggling to rise above my own performance anxiety and was simply unable to support her. She was visibly hurt and never returned to her lessons with me. Although the situation was regrettable and probably understandable, I was confused and distressed at the dilemma in which I had found myself and decided to stop teaching for the next twelve months to contemplate if it was possible to align my competitive and ambitious nature with the demands and responsibilities of teaching. I decided that it was, and began to see the necessity and benefits of these kinds of experiences and how to use them to my advantage.

In 2001, I found myself standing in the middle of a stage at the height of my career knowing that this part of my life had come to an end. I had achieved my goal of becoming an *Operatic Diva* but had never been able to embrace my success or perform without debilitating fear and insecurity. Negative emotional patterns were showing no sign of resolution and I was unable to practice much of what I was preaching to my students. In that moment I knew that I needed to stop performing to take stock of all that was out of balance and all that was keeping me from the joyful expression of who and what I truly wanted to be. This continues to be an unfolding journey for me that twists, turns, and deepens with the precious and inevitable gift of hindsight, wisdom and time.

I am continually humbled by the elevated position in which my students and colleagues place me, but it is when I am given the credit for another's *light* that I must quote, "You can lead a horse to water but you *cannot* make him drink." No matter how comprehensive or *right* the advice or information being given, not all who hear it are willing or able to adopt or utilise its wisdom. Only those who are ready for change and hold a passionate desire to shift from where they are will do so. We should not be so quick to separate those who teach from those who are being taught as, although I stand in a position of authority, it is clear to me that by attending to the needs of my students, I am also attending to my own.

NOTES:

2

LIFE'S A PITCH
The Genesis of Sound

"In the beginning there was sound, and in that sound is you."
- A. Colliver

When learning the skill of singing, it is easy to forget that we have probably uttered every single one of the sounds we are trying to make somewhere, sometime in our daily lives. Under analysis, innate actions like speech or singing suddenly become complex and difficult due to the fact that we are unaware of the way sound formulates itself and just how natural the process really is. Each of us is governed by the same physical and emotional *needs* and these needs are fulfilled via the five senses of sight, sound, taste, touch and hearing. Whatever is experienced through these senses tends to express itself through a multitude of sounds. A scream of panic, a sigh of pleasure, a shriek of laughter, a moan of pain, a whisper of love, the whine of a hungry child, a sob, the grunting of exertion, a cry of abandonment and the gasp of horror, are just a few of the faces it presents, but the crucial thing to understand is that at the most primal level, our ability to give voice to these experiences ensures our survival. This being so, makes the act of *voiced sound* innate. This innate capacity however, becomes veiled and complex when the influences of cultural conditioning are taken into consideration.

When we are babies, screaming or crying is the accepted form of communication until we are able to form and articulate words but long before we speak, each of us is learning the rules of language and sensing how our parents or role models are using it to communicate with one another. As we begin to articulate and formulate sentences, the dynamic range of our natural voices is already going through a process of modification or suppression in alignment with our family and cultural sensibilities. This layer of vocal modification is not generally recognised or understood, and so would explain why so many singers question their ability to breathe, support, project, pitch, animate, articulate and resonate their voices. Put simply, the voices we are using are often *compromised* versions of the voices we are born with, so if we are to reinstate them to their natural unadulterated state, we must first understand how they have been influenced whilst growing up.

Those from countries where cultural expression is grounded in music do not seem to face the same vocal phobias as those who are not. What I have discovered is that removing these deeply ingrained layers is not as simple as it sounds, as many of these layers are subtle and seemingly insignificant. Being Australian, I grew up in an environment of gregarious, energetic, opinionated people who found no real difficulty voicing discontent or rallying in the streets to protect the democratic rights of their family and friends. Artistic expression of all kinds was supported by the educational system, and successful performers were elevated alongside politicians, entrepreneurs and humanitarians. Nothing had prepared me for the vocal suppression I was to encounter when I relocated to Singapore in 2004 to take a full time teaching position at one of the international arts schools. Although this country takes enormous pride in cleanliness, safety, practicality and functionality, creative and energetic inertia seems to be the human trade off for it. Magnificent theatres and performing spaces have sprung up all over the country and yet there is not *one* busker to be found performing on the street corners. These theatres are proudly showcasing world-renowned artists and shows from across the globe, and yet choosing a career in the arts is not generally supported or encouraged. This, I have discovered, is only one of the reasons for the vocal difficulties singers here face, the major contributor being the lowered vocal dynamic with which many Asian countries communicate. This cultural sensibility encourages only the lower frequencies of sound, neglecting virtually all of the upper range. The higher notes are informed by extreme emotions like passion, joy, laughter and rage, which are an essential part of communication, so if these emotions are absent or suppressed, the vocal result is an unnaturally shortened range, tonal dullness and physical disconnect.

Many singers experience vocal issues because of a failure to understand that singing must be extended from every sound and every pitch with which they communicate. But, because the lower frequencies are more utilised and relevant to daily communication, the importance of the extreme emotions like screaming and yelling are almost completely neglected. The market vendor, however, has no difficulty setting his voice at the cutting pitch necessary to sell his wares, as his survival depends on being heard above the rabble of the market place. Although vocal suppression is more pronounced in certain parts of Asia, it should be noted that it is still a universal malaise.

I remember the day Sarah, a petite 16-year-old ballerina, walked into my studio and pragmatically stated, "I don't have any high notes and my vocal range is really small." I promptly asked her if she were being attacked and was in real danger, did she think she would be able to scream. "Definitely", she said. I then asked her if she realised that when she screamed to protect herself she would access all the high notes she thought she didn't have, and if she were to hold them and then add vibrato she would be singing. Sarah appeared confused and shook her head. In less than half an hour Sarah had extended her upper range by more than five notes by pretending she was about to scream. She was shocked and wanted to know how she could have done this so quickly. I told her that I had simply helped her to set up the *emotional conditions* she would naturally use for survival, which immediately guaranteed her those notes.

In the words of Richard Strauss, *"The human voice is the most beautiful instrument of all but is the most difficult to play"*. So why is this I wonder? The answer is simple; because the human body is at the mercy of the intellect and the emotions. When the focus of the mind is on survival, the *conditioned* part of the brain unknowingly steps aside, allowing the *intuitive* body to take over.

One of the hardest things for singers to do is to see themselves as a human *vessel or conduit for sound* when they are singing, rather than a *person* or a *personality*. Obviously, we *are* people with personalities but when this perspective takes over and begins to dominate, it is easy to go against the natural workings of the body. Vocal technique is often perceived to be 'added layers of conceptual knowledge', and conscious muscle manipulation rather than *a deep understanding of how the human instrument works*. I am continually dismayed at the amount of unnecessary work singers undertake in the belief that they are actually helping themselves. Even with physiological understanding it is impossible to see our own vocal process at work, so any attempt to measure or manually manipulate sound will interrupt the delicate balance that exists among the *physical, mental* and *emotional* bodies. That being said, it can be extremely useful to work on these three areas independently to highlight and explore technical problems using specific exercises to support and rectify any difficulties being experienced. It is only when any *one* of these three areas is seen to be *the* answer on its own that there can be serious technical repercussions that are often difficult to pinpoint or resolve.

One general misunderstanding among singers is that there is one generic shape for each vowel sound. But when we look at speech patterns, we will find that when in the lower range the mouth shapes become smaller, and when in the higher range more space is required. Subsequently, the breathing, support, placement, range, tone, volume and projection organise themselves according to the requirements of the result, and the emotions that are motivating the sounds, are naturally creating the correct degree of muscular activity.

Although each individual will describe it differently, there are definite sensations connected to a sound that is well placed and flowing freely, just as there are definite emotions connected to upper and lower frequencies. Higher notes are informed by extreme emotions like passion, joy, laughter and rage, and lower notes by more intimate and speech like intentions. The only way of accessing a reliable vocal result is to understand the *motivation* and subsequent *sensation* of the sounds you are trying to create, which moves the emphasis away from external manipulation towards the internal interchange going on between the mind and the body.

Becoming aware of something we have always done unconsciously is no easy feat, and knowing intellectually that we are born with a palate of vocal colours and the innate understanding of how to use them is not enough to create the action of singing. Without consistent observation and exploration of ourselves and of others physically, emotionally, and intellectually, much of the potential we hold within our voices remains untapped and unrealised. Becoming self-aware and observant in our daily lives allows us to catch sight of the thought processes and habits that prevent us from claiming the voice that is truly ours.

Exercises:

a) *Take the time to watch someone who is laughing, crying, yelling or screaming, and notice what effect the emotion has on the pitch of his or her voice. Is it high, is it low, is it free, is it joyful or fearful, and how are these emotions affecting his or her body? Is the person self-conscious or embracing the energy fully? Does it look natural or awkward?*

b) *Observe yourself in the same way when you sing. Are you tense or are you breathing easily? Is your body feeling agitated or calm? Are you pacing or are you standing still? Is your mind wandering? Are you able to feel your voice flowing easily and freely, or is it feeling constricted? Do you know what vocal results you are trying to achieve, and are you achieving them? If not, do you have another vocal option?*

c) *Listen to the voices of your parents and friends. What do they sound like? Do you think you speak the same way they do? Are their vocal dynamics loud or soft? Is the tone monotonous or does it vary in colour? Can you sense what kind of mood they're in by the way they produce the sound? Do you find their vocal quality attractive? If not, do you have any opinion on what they might do to improve the sound?*

d) *Experiment with your expression and its effect on the sound by singing high notes with a dead face and low notes with exaggerated animation. Feel how the high notes become flat and swallowed without the correct emotion and how the low notes feel disconnected and almost impossible to resonate when the face is emulating an emotion that is too extreme for the pitch you are on.*

e) *Get into the habit of recording everything you do, as what you are hearing in your head is only around 60% of the sound being made. Acknowledge the sounds you like and analyse what they feel like and how you achieve them. Now begin to apply this sensation to any of the sounds that fall short of this result.*

NOTES:

3

BREATHING:
The Ins and Outs of it

"Learn to exhale, the inhalation will take care of itself"
- Carla Melucci

Before you begin this chapter, take a few minutes to focus on the way you are breathing in this particular moment. Does it feel high and constricted, is it shallow, uneven, or laboured, are you holding your breath, is the air audible when you inhale, do you feel slightly breathless, or, does your abdomen feel as if it releases, allowing the air to flow deeply, calmly and evenly into your body? Take another moment to consider if the way you breathe changes from day to day. If the answer is yes, how does it change and under what emotional circumstances does this happen? If you find you have never really paid much attention to any or all of these questions, it is time that you do.

I don't recall my teachers asking me to pay much attention to the way I breathed when I was training to be a singer, which could either have been a massive oversight on their part, or simply due to the fact that I was already competently controlling and utilising my breath when I sang. Classical singing has more than a tendency to trigger the complex network of muscular co-ordinations necessary for breath management, and the repertoire I was tackling simply could not have been negotiated without at least some of the necessary support being in place. One thing I do remember, however, was being taken aside after an audition by a well-known singing teacher who bluntly told me that she thought I was vocally working too hard, and rather than focusing on the air I was taking in, perhaps I should concentrate more on *how* and even more importantly, *if* that air was moving freely out of my body. This was more than food for thought for me, and has influenced the way I approach the subject of breath control with my own students. Another influencing moment was when I attended a workshop with Jo Estill who, although extremely knowledgeable and well researched in anatomy and the relationship between breathing and the voice, refused to address the issue of breath support directly by saying, "If the upper body is released and the sound is clear and free, the supporting muscles will be doing all the right things." This approach resonated strongly with me, and the "as above, so below" philosophy has worked extremely well in my teaching practice and with my own voice.

In my initial consultation with a new student, I always ask what kind of vocal problems he or she is experiencing. More often than not, one of the answers will be, "I don't know how to breathe." This is obviously an exaggeration as there are no difficulties with their ability to inhale and exhale, so what they really mean is, "The way I'm breathing doesn't give me the vocal results I want." This immediately tells me that the problem does not lie in the student's capacity to breathe, but rather in the way the breath is being taken in, converted to sound and projected. Many singers do not understand that the human body is only the *vehicle* through which sound passes, just as a hose is the vehicle through which water is delivered. If the hose becomes twisted, the water becomes trapped, losing pressure and momentum, preventing its natural and energetic flow. The same applies to sound, in that if air is *compromised* as it is drawn in, the throat becomes constricted and sound cannot pass through the body cleanly, strongly or evenly.

It is easy to understand why we have little or no awareness of this process, as breathing is an automatic reflex action, and it is not necessary to consciously manipulate it to stay alive - but if this breath is to remain uncompromised as it travels through the body, conscious awareness of the way the air is being utilised becomes crucial for a singer. However, the intrinsic simplicity of air traveling in and out of the body can become complex due to its resilience to being bullied and forced whilst still continuing to do the job of keeping us alive and allowing us to produce sound. This simple fact sees many of us focusing more on the *voiced* sound, without realising that what we are hearing is a *symptom* of the way the air has been *taken in* and *sent out*.

Singing is an intricate and delicate balance of *tension* and *release*, the challenge being how to create *tension without constriction* and *release without collapse.* Just as I have witnessed those with no ability to create the energy necessary for a grounded or anchored sound, so have I also known those who take unnecessary control of the muscular co-ordinations that the body would otherwise be doing for itself. This places a direct spotlight on the need for some kind of clarification of the term *breath control*.

Are you in control or being controlling?
The word *control* has several connotations depending on the context in which it is being used, and is a word that can confuse and frustrate singers when they are learning to tread the fine line of what to do and what not to do. The kind of control used to manipulate inanimate objects or external matter is not the same kind of control that involves tuning into the subtleties of energy (air) and going with its *flow*. In other words, when using inanimate objects like a remote control or a hand phone, you must manipulate or control these objects externally, but when you are skiing down a slope or skydiving, there will be a sense of *freefall* or being out of control where you must allow the momentum of the action to carry you. Muscle manipulation occurs *within* this freefall, but must never interrupt it. To do this, however, you must understand what results you are trying to achieve and set up an *intention* to execute them. Only when those results are manifested can you be sure that you are using the right kind of control.

> ## "Power is the capacity to translate intention into reality and then sustain it."
> *- Warren Bennis*

Precise action only has the possibility of occurring if there is a clear *intention*. Your body is responding to your emotions, your emotions are responding to your intention, and your intention is dictating the way in which the air travels through your body. Unless your intention is clear and informed, the vocal outcome cannot be reliable. To implement an intention you must know what your choices are, and to have choices you must understand the nature of what it is you are making choices about. It is not enough to know that the correct intake of air needs to be *low* or *anchored*, or that *compromised* air is often *clavicular* or *high*. Instead, you must understand *why* the air is manifesting in this way and work your way back to the *cause*. Intention, at its most basic level, happens naturally through verbal communication where emotions dictate the pitch, expression, and the level of air needed to support them. Things only become difficult in singing if the fundamental principles of speech are removed, so it is vital to understand that if the action of singing is not supported by an intention to *speak*, the breath will organise itself unnaturally.

Exercises:

a) Stop and take five minutes either to sit comfortably, or to lie down in a way that enables you to tune into the way you are breathing in this particular moment. Place one hand on your solar plexus and one below the navel, observing the rise and fall of your abdomen and the release of the pelvic area. Now take your awareness to the place you are drawing the air from, and feel its journey from your intention to breathe, to its entry into your lungs, to its exhalation out of your body, and then create the intention to repeat the same action again. By repeating this three or four times, you will begin to tune into the order in which the action of breathing is happening, and will begin to find yourself more in control of your breath without external manipulation.

b) Continue lying down and repeat the same exercise, but this time as you exhale, allow the air to become a sound. Choose any pitch or a simple tune, and create a musical phrase with the same intention you were using in the voiceless exercise. Notice the muscular contraction you feel in your abdomen and pelvis and begin to associate it with the sound you are making.

c) Try the same two exercises while standing and see if you can achieve and maintain the same result you were getting when you were lying down.

The more the merrier?

One common misconception among singers is the belief that the more air you inhale, the longer the phrases you will be able to sustain, and the more sound or volume you will be able to create. Unfortunately, it's not quite as simplistic as this, as the amount of air needed for any particular phrase will vary according to the tessitura or pitch of the music and the level of difficulty of the phrase being sung. For example, if you draw in copious amounts of air for a short phrase with many low notes, the inhalation is acting as though it is about to sing a long phrase with high notes, making it overly animated, constricted and not at all relevant to the musical circumstances. You simply *do not* need this amount of air and your voice will not tolerate this "one size fits all" approach. It is the *absence of escaping air* that creates tonal quality, so if the inhalation is overdone, unnecessary pressure is created behind the vocal folds as they hold back the air in an attempt to create tone, much like a dam holding back a wall of water. To get the best out of your air supply you must learn to *budget* what you inhale. Your support system will collapse if you expend it all on the first few notes of a phrase and will lock if you do not allow a consistent exhalation to occur. This makes the delicate balance between inhalation and exhalation the ultimate challenge for a singer.

Despite physiological facts, diagrams, and innovative explanations, analysis of the vocal process cannot suffice on its own, so I will continue to remind you that as these variables are impossible to measure, they can only be organised by the correct vocal result. Therefore it is imperative that you understand how the air *feels* as it enters and exits your body and the type of vocal result those sensations are producing for you. Only then can you expect to recreate the correct result with any kind of consistency.

One activity I find very effective with my students is to ask them to do things incorrectly, which subsequently highlights what they are doing unconsciously, providing tangible opposing sensations that can help them correct the mistakes they are making.

Exercises:

a) *Take a low musical phrase from a song in your repertoire and try to sing it after taking an overly animated breath. Ask yourself how it feels. Is the tonal quality breathy? Is the pitch a little sharp? Does the sound feel disconnected and weak? Is the phrase uneven and difficult to control? Can you successfully create volume or does the sound fall away when you apply energy to it?*

b) *Now speak the phrase and observe how much air is necessary to create the tonal quality of what you are saying. Then create exactly the same preparation but instead of speaking, sing. Is the result different this time? Is there more tone in the sound and is the pitch better? Can you energize it more easily and does it feel as though it is anchored lower in your body?*

c) *In exactly the same way, take a high musical phrase and try to sing it using the under animated breath you used for the lower phrase. Did you mange to reach the notes or was it flat in pitch? Was it difficult to maintain a consistent feeling of control?*

d) *Now speak the phrase at a higher pitch and in a far more animated manner (this can be done in both registers). Again, observe the way you needed to breathe to achieve this and apply it to the vocal phrase. Analyse the results and arrive at your own conclusion as to whether or not the amount of air you needed for the low tessitura and high tessitura were different.*

e) *Record yourself doing the exercises and then listen back to them. You will gain a more truthful picture of the results when you can be an audience member to yourself. Decide which of the sounds are correct and try to make them part of your intention every time you sing.*

Ready, set, go

The point at which air passes over the vocal folds and is converted into audible sound is called a *vocal onset*. This onset can manifest in several different ways and offer valuable insight into how the air has been inspired, directed and released at the beginning of the voiced action. The onset is responsible for setting up the entire phrase and, if done correctly, will resolve a multitude of technical difficulties.

- A *glottal* or *hard* onset is one that interrupts the conversion process due to the closure of the glottis before the sound occurs. This is symptomatic of inhaling air too early and holding it momentarily before creating the sound. The singer must understand that the inhaled air is going to become the sound the *moment* it passes over the vocal folds, so unless this air is converted without interruption, *legato line* will never be successfully achieved. Glottal onsets definitely have their place in all styles of music but should never be used in the foundational technical work (scales, vocalises).

- The *aspirate* or *soft* onset is created by allowing air to escape before the tone begins, which is symptomatic of insufficient energy to close the vocal folds. The result is a breathy tonal quality and although it has an effective place in the styles of jazz and pop, flatness of pitch and collapsing support muscles are a direct casualty of this type of vocal onset.

- The *simultaneous* or *uninterrupted* onset is achieved when the air seamlessly becomes the sound with no apparent entry point. Just like the elements of air, water, and fire, sound can be interrupted or shut down at the *source,* but its nature is to flow continuously. A *swing* or a *pendulum* can serve as wonderful visuals for the seamless journey from the inhalation to the exhalation that is necessary for correct vocal placement and legato line.

Exercises:

a) Stand in front of a mirror and say, "Ah." Take note of whether you breathe slightly too early, creating a glottal stop before it, or whether the sound is a direct and uninterrupted extension of your breath. If confused, try creating the sound with a glottal stop first and then attempt to onset the sound without an audible break. After achieving this correctly with speech, you can attempt to do the same by singing the same sound.

b) Repeat the same exercise with an aspirated, or breathy, onset by allowing the air to escape as you onset the sound. Feel the weakness, collapse, and lack of presence in this sound and then try to remove the airiness from your next attempt.

c) If you are managing to avoid a glottal stop before you sing, you will be achieving what is known as a simultaneous or uninterrupted onset or, in other words, no bump in the road or hiccup when you start. This type of onset engages the correct amount of abdominal support for vocal placement and feels very different to the others. Pay attention to the sensation in your lower body (it will be abdominally more demanding) and compare it to the flaccid sensation of the breathy onset and the hard, jolting feeling of the glottal onset done previously.

Making the unconscious *conscious*
Although the automatic action of breathing serves us well at the most basic level, many of us are only utilising a portion of its potential offerings. Stress encourages shallow breathing, which, for a singer, sets up a disastrous pattern of inconsistent vocal outcomes by tightening the abdomen, preventing the diaphragm from descending, and creating tension and constriction in the muscles of the neck. Learning to *breathe with awareness* offers invaluable benefits to each of us, both vocally and in our daily lives, but unless we hold a deep interest and hunger to know more, these benefits will remain unrecognised and unexplored. Yoga, tai chi, and meditational practices aid the development of body awareness and self-esteem, and all have a similar aim of bringing us into the present moment and away from the projections of an unknowable future and the prison of the past. This, in turn, allows the breath to slow down, creating a state of relaxation, confidence, and peace. Unfortunately, although theses practices are vital for our health and well-being, they are often considered to be too *alternative* or *new age* for mainstream use, leaving them severely underutilised or simply a last resort when all else fails.

Suggested Practices:

The Alexander Technique, Feldenkrais, ATM (Awareness Through Movement), The Buteyko Method, Pranayama Yoga

If these are not options for you, simply try to become aware of the way you breathe in your daily life and, where necessary, practice changing the state of your thoughts and observe the effect it has on your body and your breath. This will help you understand that you are, in fact, calling the shots and are also the creator of all your physical responses.

Air is an invisible force, as is the sound it creates. It cannot be held, but it is tangible. It decays in a moment, and yet the experience of it remains. It can disappear, but can be resurrected again with a single thought and a clear decision. Conceptual analysis and physiology will provide you with answers on the *ins and outs* and the *how to* of breathing, but the human instrument is constantly in a state of action and reaction, so the answers are not only found in the complex web of our thoughts and emotions but, most importantly, how they translate physically.

Suggested reading on Anatomy/physiology:

- Hixon, T.J. 2006. *Respiratory Function in Singing: A Primer for Singers and Singing Teachers.* Tucson: Redington Brown.

- McCoy, S. 2004. *Your Voice: An Inside View.* Princeton: Inside View Press.

- Melton, J. 2009. *"Ab Prints and the Triple Threat,"* NYSTA Newsletter, NYC.

- Melton J., Tom, K. 2012. *One Voice: Integrating Singing and Theatre Voice Techniques.* Long Grove, IL: Waveland.

- Titze, I.R. 2000. *Principles of Voice Production.* Salt Lake City: National Center for Voice and Speech.

NOTES:

4

THE RAINBOW GATHERING
It Takes All Kinds

"Share the similarities and celebrate the differences."
- M. Scott Peck

Have you ever imagined a rainbow with only one colour? It simply wouldn't be a rainbow would it? No one colour can ever be deemed more important than the other, as they all contribute equally to this awe-inspiring phenomenon. In celebration of this fact, festivals known as *Rainbow Gatherings* are regularly held around the world to embrace and celebrate the ideals of love, peace, freedom, individuality, and community. Embracing our own individuality is not always easy and is only possible if we can believe that we all have something unique to offer.

What is it that defines who we really are? Is it our race, culture, family, friends, vocation, and our skills, or is it our dreams, aspirations, feelings, life experience, and our innate capacity to love and be loved? There is a contradictory cultural *bent* in Australia known as the "Tall Poppy Syndrome," which is the description of a successful person or *tall poppy,* that becomes the target of jealousy and derogatory remarks in an attempt to cut him or her down to the level of the masses. This way, the benchmark remains low and the inadequacies and failures of others are not so obvious. In stark contrast, Australians are also renowned and revered for their *Mateship*, and pride themselves on equality, loyalty, generosity, and friendship. In my opinion, when in crisis, you'll find no greater ability or willingness to come to the rescue of another anywhere else in the world and that, I believe, is representative of the true heart of my country.

All of us are casualties of some form of cultural negativity, but it is easy to lose sight of the fact that sexist, racist, classist, and ageist views are exactly that - simply perceptions and attitudes, but not in any way the truth about life and all its possibilities. Intuition and imagination, on the other hand, hover as endless sources of creative potential, and when called upon, inspire us to levels of greatness despite our conditioning. Over the years I have encountered many different *artistic energies*, but I have never met anyone who did not have a quality that could potentially benefit or contribute to another. Believing this however, becomes an ongoing challenge for those who do not consider themselves to be attractive or gifted.

No matter what generation we have been brought up in, all of us have been subjected to stereotypes of one kind or another, but never has the pressure to appear ageless and unblemished been stronger than it is today. For most of us, this kind of unrealistic expectation is not sustainable and as long as we fall into the trap of trying to accommodate it, we can never really experience the joyful rewards of living from our own authenticity.

Although intrinsically true, phrases such as, "Just be yourself," "Beauty is in the eye of the beholder," and "It's what's on the inside that counts," have become glib and meaningless clichés in a society that has many of us believing that confidence and safety are found in the comparing of ourselves to others. This almost always has the opposite effect, serving only to highlight our weaknesses, perpetuating disillusionment and confusion. On the other hand, measuring ourselves against someone or something that elevates us to become a better version of ourselves is completely different and makes the act of comparison constructive, inspirational, and motivating. *Energy moves and morphs* as we grow and change and, although our character traits remain fundamentally the same, we all have the capacity to balance what is imbalanced, to temper what is overbearing, and to nourish what is underdeveloped or damaged. To do this we must understand and accept the things we cannot change and set about changing the things we can.

A few weeks ago a friend of mine wanted to introduce me to an organic farm he had discovered on the outskirts of Singapore known as "Bollywood," but most of all, he wanted me to meet Ivy. An imposing but gregarious middle-aged woman, Ivy stood in the warrior pose with her arms crossed, legs apart and hunting knife strapped to her waist. Notorious for her protection of the environment, fighting for the underdog, political incorrectness, and colourful language, Ivy was eager to embark on an inflammatory conversation about her latest humanitarian conquest with my friend the minute we arrived.

Then I met May. Some people are impossible to describe, so I will simply say that May was the most unchallenged *challenged* person I had ever met. May was thirty-two years old, the Bollywood kitchen hand, published author, and cerebral palsy sufferer. She flew towards us with the agility of someone who was completely at home in her twisted body, smiling broadly and bantering with intelligence and wit, joyfully took our lunch orders, and then promptly disappeared. Halfway through our meal, May burst out of the kitchen sporting a glittering crown of Christmas decorations, melodramatically slicing the air with a fairy wand and laughing like the sun. I was utterly mesmerised by the purity of the energy dancing before me and, as she spun around blissfully basking in the warmth of her own light, I knew that I had never seen anything or anyone as beautiful.

Many things were put into perspective for me that day as I was reminded that the labels of *plain, small, old, challenged* or *unconventional* are of no real significance where there is acceptance and love. People like Ivy and May don't just magically arrive at some preordained destination but, rather, they know who they are and how they wish to live their lives. This particular kind of authenticity is often found in those who have had to deal with extreme adversity, but thankfully we do not have to experience the same degree of difficulty to develop the same remarkable qualities.

It's pointless to feel guilty that you have sight and someone else is blind, or that you have shelter and food and someone else does not. There is, however, a point to valuing and constructively using what you have been given, because despite your physical, mental, and emotional imperfections, there will always be someone, somewhere who would give anything to have some of what you have.

"A goal without a plan is just a wish."
- Antoine de Saint-Exupery

If we wish to achieve anything of significance in our lives, we must firstly have a *plan of action* that is in alignment with the goals we have in mind. In my experience, performers tend to be more intuitive and creative than they are logical, analytical, and objective, and therefore can be naïve or complacent when it comes to *strategy* and *action*. I was one such person.

Although I had attended countless life coaching seminars and self-empowerment courses over the years, I had only managed to integrate a portion of the gathered information. The rest of it hung like a beautiful but elusive cobweb in my mind waiting for its moment of *glory*. True to the saying,

"When the student is ready, the teacher will arrive", I recently found myself attending a series of courses (*Shine, Evolve, Bloom*) at a place called the SoulCentre in Singapore. These courses are created and run by the internationally renowned and much-loved mentor Vikas Malkani whose affable, bear like persona, and penchant for imparting spiritual truth via simple and heart warming stories, brings simplicity and lightness to subjects that, for many of us, are almost indigestible. Over the years, I have experienced many paradigm-shifting moments, but it was the following life coaching strategy that I learned from him which has become a lynchpin for my knowledge and my understanding of how to take action in my own life.

From the time we are born to the time of our death, our lives consist of three things only: *being*, *doing*, and *having*. Most of us make the mistake of dwelling on what it is we want to *have* without realising that before *having* something is possible, there are things we firstly need to *be* and *do*. *Being* is the attitude with which we *do* something, and the way in which we *do* things allows us to *have* what it is we want. This is the order in which *manifestation* occurs.

Questions - Begin by asking yourself these questions, keeping them specific to your musical goals:

1. *Who do I want to be in my life? (Feelings and attitudes, e.g., strong, confident, charismatic, positive, successful)*

2. *What do I need to do in order to be that? (Action, e.g., find a life coach/teacher, sign up for an online course, attend master-classes and workshops to further my knowledge and expertise, learn to pinpoint negative behavioural patterns and practice changing or modifying them throughout my daily life)*

3. *What do I want to have? (Material possessions, e.g., status, life experiences, e.g., a solid vocal technique, a professional singing career, to write and record an album)*

Being (feelings)
The words we use carry energy and serve as an immediate reflection of our thoughts and attitudes which, in turn, dictate how we are perceived and treated by others.

No buts about it
Sentences such as, "I really want to pursue a career in singing, but..", "I know I have the talent to be successful, but..", "My technical ability is so much better than it was, but.." are defeatist, and even without completing the sentences it is clear that there will be an excuse as to why the student cannot have what she or he wants. If we look closely at the first half of the sentence, we see that the positive statement of the student's desire to *have* is quickly negated by the second half of the sentence when his or her inability to take action, or to *do*, manifests as the word *but*. However, if we change the word *but* to *so,* the energy of the sentence becomes positive and hopeful, prompting us to ask the questions of *what, when, how* and *why*, which lead to the actions that will give us the things we wish to *have*.

Exercise:

Make up a few of your own sentences firstly using the word *but*, and then the word *so*. For example:

"I am working hard on my technique, *but* I never seem to improve."

"I am working hard on my technique, *so* what do I need to do to improve?"

> **"The road to success is dotted with many tempting parking places."**
> *- Will Rogers*

Doing (action)
Taking action is where so many of us can become *stuck*, as inspiring and motivating ideas are so easily postponed or placed on the shelf when there is insufficient clarity about what it is we truly want to achieve. Put simply, if you know what you want and you want it badly enough, you will find the ways and means to take the appropriate action.

- Be realistic and clear about what it is you want.

- Find the mentors who can guide and teach you.

- Take personal responsibility for your own success and never give up.

Having (material possessions, life experiences, status)
Achieving your goals and getting what you want will have its own set of challenges. Many times I have seen performers fight for prestigious roles and elevated positions in the industry only to complain about the pressure and commitment when the novelty of achieving them has worn off. If you love what you do and are sure it is what you want, the joy of doing it will always outweigh the difficulties and obstacles you will invariably encounter. Achieving status and success is one thing, but building on your knowledge and maintaining your position takes ongoing diligence, courage, and tenacity.

- Be grateful for your success.

- Become independent of others by creating your own opportunities.

- Continue to expand your knowledge and skills.

- Learn to outsource to those who have expertise in the areas you do not.

- Regularly assess whether or not what you are doing makes you happy. If it does not, take necessary steps to change the situation.

Differences between people would not and could not exist unless there were a purpose and a place for them all. Take a close look at those you consider to be charismatic and successful, and you will see that they are not superficial stereotypes, but authentic individuals who passionately follow the vision they have for themselves. Therefore, the only questions you need to ask yourself are what do you want to *have,* and what must you *be* and *do* to have it. All other things will follow.

5

THE X FACTOR
You Either Have It or You Don't

"There are only 3 colors, 10 digits and 7 notes. It is what we do with them that's important."

- Jim Rohn

THE X FACTOR

One sunny Melbourne afternoon, Hugh arrived at my studio for his first singing lesson. He had just been cast as the romantic lead of Gaston in the Australian production of *Beauty and the Beast*, although he was already an accomplished actor, he had never seriously taken singing lessons. I was immediately taken by his raw vocal talent, affable nature, and stunning good looks, but more than that, he seemed to possess wisdom unusual for a young man of 25. A few minutes into the lesson I experienced a surreal moment when I heard myself say, "I hope you're ready to become a superstar," at which point he looked at me, smiled, and without a trace of vanity replied, "I think I am." Hugh suffered the same vocal difficulties all singers do, but every challenge was met with a sense of humour and more than a strong penchant for adventure. I worked closely with him over the next two years and literally watched him decide what kind of person he wanted to be, whom he was going to marry, where he wanted to live, and the kind of career he wanted to have - which has seen him become one of the most respected and versatile performers in the industry today. As many of us know, he is one of the most acclaimed Hollywood superstars in the world but, despite his phenomenal success, he remains as humble today as he was when I first met him.

I have often wondered exactly what it is in someone that ensures success and have come to the conclusion that when individuals know who they are, what they believe, and what it is they wish to achieve in life, they have an *energy* or *light* that is charismatic, powerful and attractive. It is this energy or light that is commonly labeled the *X factor*. Unfortunately, along with this enigma comes the general belief that "You either have it or you don't." What exactly it is that one does or doesn't have is the source of endless debate. It is undeniably true that some individuals are more in touch with their creative impulses than others, but this phenomenon should not negate the fact that every one of us is a *being of unlimited power and potential*, and perhaps, when it is not apparent or visible, it simply highlights the fact that we are all at different stages of development and have not yet *come into our own*.

Just over a year ago, a rather unremarkable, overweight, and extremely self-conscious 17-year-old boy called Frank walked into my studio and asked me if I would take him on as my student. He did not appear to have much going for him other than a passionate dream to forge a professional career in musical theatre, but I was later to find out that he possessed the kind of tenacity and courage particular to those who succeed in life. Unlike most Chinese-Singaporeans, he did not live with his parents as the moment he had announced his musical aspirations to his family, his father had banished him from the house in disgust. His mother had been placed in the impossible position of choosing between her husband and her son but, despite her own misgivings about Frank's scholastic choices, was secretly paying for his singing lessons in an attempt to support his dreams. One particular day he came into his lesson shaken and distressed. His father had just told him in no uncertain terms that he was delusional if he thought he could ever be a good singer, and that he would never forgive him for the deep and personal betrayal of his family and his culture or, for that matter, ever come to see him perform. Frank came close to giving up his dream that day, but resumed his lessons the following week with renewed clarity and commitment. In the weeks to come a more joyful and confident young man began to emerge, revealing a promising Baritone voice and an individuality and charisma not previously visible. It is obvious that Hugh and Frank are extremely different people at radically different stages of creative development, and on completely different journeys, but it is the understanding and acceptance that this is a natural and normal process that allows us to move towards the things we want for ourselves at our own pace.

One primary malaise of the 21st century is the intolerance for the natural growth process, exacerbated by the addiction to instant gratification. This is breeding an insidious kind of impatience whereby plants, animals, food, and people are being pushed into developing faster than is natural, and has become so widely accepted that it is increasingly difficult to find a creative environment free of the subliminal message that *time is running out*. Unfortunately, this only serves to encourage us to tackle things we are not ready for, which leads us to an unrealistic perception and often pessimistic view of where we lie in our own development. The next time you're in a garden, take a look at the flowers growing there. Some will be in the embryonic stages of growth, unseen beneath the soil, some will be just beginning to peep through the earth, some will be buds not yet fully opened, some will be flowers in full, glorious bloom, and some will be plants that are past their prime and in a state of decline or decay. Most certainly the one that draws your attention will be the flower in full bloom, but take a moment to look at the others not yet open, and consider if you believe that they too will eventually have their time of glory in the garden.

> **"No one is ordinary and uninspiring; we simply learn to be that way"**
> *- A Colliver*

At one time or another we all find ourselves in a *rut*, be it in our jobs, relationships, or in the way we view ourselves and others and, when we do, we are suffering from a lack of what is commonly known as *inspiration*. Interestingly, this word has two meanings: *stimulation leading to heightened emotions,* and *to inhale air*. Heightened emotions stimulate *action* and the inhalation of air guarantees us *life*, so it is easy to see that if there is no inspiration, there is no life. If, indeed, we are all energetic beings of unlimited power and potential, how do we so often find ourselves suffering the quagmire of inertia? The most obvious answer is that we are not conditioned to credit ourselves with unlimited power and potential, and therefore do not always know what we're capable of achieving. Even if we are aware of our own capabilities, it is often unclear where we can go for help if and when we find ourselves uninspired or unmotivated. This kind of apathy accumulates over time, and eventually leads to a kind of creative impasse.

Reality television preys on this kind of human apathy by offering the very thing we all need to survive - *hope*. Hope occurs when we see something we want, on one hand believing that it may not be possible to achieve, but on the other hand believing that it might be. Whether it be the *hope* to lose weight, the *hope* to find a loving and lasting relationship, the *hope* to become rich and famous, the *hope* to be the next top model, or the *hope* to be told that you are special and possess the coveted *X factor*, hope is integral to life. In a nutshell, we all long for some kind of change for the better, but it appears that we need to be continually inspired by the metamorphoses of others to remind us that it is also possible for us.

In the past, the disadvantaged characters of *The Ugly Duckling, Cinderella,* and the *Frog Prince* pulled on our heartstrings and gave us hope for a better future. But now, the underdog archetypes are emulated by the obese woman who drops 100 pounds to become a stunning model, the family who have their home rebuilt from the ashes by a loving community, the plain and dowdy middle aged woman who becomes a vocal sensation overnight, and the courageous teenager who finally beats drug addiction or anorexia against all odds. Quite simply, these stories provide the inspiration and hope necessary to motivate us towards our own goals and dreams, but the danger is that we can find ourselves living our lives through the achievement of others and avoid dealing with our own particular circumstances.

Kaye is dark and impishly beautiful with a gregarious nature and quirky personality, but the state of her career has not always been reflective of the colourful and successful Diva she is today. In her first singing lesson with me I remember hearing her say that she would be happy to be in the chorus of a musical but that no one would cast her. I was more than bemused when I heard her sing, as she possessed a voice and a personality that would have been completely wasted in a chorus. I told her that she seriously needed to raise her expectations for herself and become the star she already was. The next time I saw her she was performing to packed houses in a sellout season of her own cabaret show, where she was bringing the house down with her perverse sense of humor and immense vocal talent. Several years later Kaye has paid her dues, and is not only an accomplished dancer, choreographer, actor, director, teacher, and writer, but has just been granted a Green Card allowing her to work in the USA. Within a few weeks of relocating to New York, she landed the lead role of Donna in the musical *Mamma Mia!* and continues her exciting and much deserved successes to this day. Kaye still gives me credit for *that* lesson, labeling it a major turning point in her life, but although I gave her the inspiration she needed at that time, it was her own ability to take action that has literally made her dream a reality.

Interestingly, the term *X Factor* is idiomatic and has no real definition, but it is commonly used to describe those who stand out from the crowd because they have something *extra* that sets them apart from others. So what is this extra ingredient?

- **An X factor personality is**
  Extroverted, expressive, exuberant, extreme, exact, exemplary

- **An X factor personality is willing to**
  Experiment, explore, execute, examine, expose, extend, exceed, exaggerate, extract, expand

- **An X factor personality has**
  Expertise, experience

- **An X factor personality becomes**
  Extraordinary, exciting, exhilarating, explosive, exalted

- **An X factor personality doesn't make**
  Excuses

All of these qualities and actions are freely available and are simply an inspired by-product of joy and happiness. When we do something we love, we are happy, and when we are happy, energy becomes positively magnified, and when energy is positively magnified, it becomes a bright and shining beacon, which draws others to its light. If we are able to see that success comes from *doing what we love*, it then becomes clear that success lies in *loving what we do*. Hugh, Frank and Kaye are all doing what they love and continue to do it without apology or excuse. In my eyes, this *exalts* them all.

Seeking encouragement and support is part of the human condition which, if denied, becomes the major contributor to insecurity and mediocrity. To tell a sapling that it will never become a tree is to stunt its growth, just as to tell students that they do not have the capacity to powerfully express themselves is to discourage them from exploration and discovery. On the other hand, it is equally detrimental to tell a sapling that it has already become a tree or to tell students that they are capable of executing things of which they are not. A healthy combination of realism and idealism is in order, where you not only understand your current level of capability but also have aspirations to improve them and become greater. Many have not grown up in an environment of validation or creative stimulus, and are therefore unaware that the perception they have of themselves has been heavily influenced by the opinions of those around them. *Energy* has no boundaries, limitation, or bias other than those that we individually or collectively place upon it. Those who communicate fearlessly understand that they have power and presence, and those who do not are simply unable to see that they too possess light, they too have the right to be heard, and they too have the ability to shine.

Exercises:

a) **Examine** *the way you approach your voice.*

b) **Expand** *your mindset by* **experimenting** *with new sounds and* **exploring** *new concepts and ideas.*

c) **Exorcise** *your fear by* **exposing** *your emotions.*

d) **Extend** *your capabilities by* **exceeding** *your* **expectations.**

e) **Execute** *your work with* **excitement, exuberance, and expression**.

f) **Exceed** *your* **expectations** *and allow yourself to be* **extraordinary**.

NOTES:

6

THE CROCODILE PIT:
An Imperfect Instrument

"Imperfection itself has its own perfect state"
- Thomas De Quincey

Knowledge gives us choices and choices give us freedom, but in a day and age when all kinds of information can freely and easily be accessed via computers or books, there is a worrying absence of *knowledge* and *freedom* being exhibited by singers. This, I believe, is due to a chronic lack of vocal exploration exacerbated not only by the irrational fears of making mistakes and publically losing face, but also by a lack of understanding that sound is a *symptom or result* of how it is handled.

Although seemingly unimportant, there is a profound difference of approach between a student who says, "I want to sing" and one who says, "I want to *learn* how to sing," as those inspired and interested in the learning process are far more capable of exploration and experimentation than those who want to arrive at the finished product as soon as possible. How can we expect to sing well if we haven't explored the range of sounds we carry within us? How do we negotiate an instrument we don't understand? How can we choose a sound we don't know we have, and how can we know the answers to the questions we haven't yet asked? It is only on the rare occasion we find talented individuals able to sing effortlessly and seamlessly throughout their range and registers without years of training, and those select few should not dissuade the rest of us from taking the necessary steps towards vocal mastery.

To be human is to be imperfect, and therefore we need to understand that when we are learning to sing we are, in fact, learning to negotiate an instrument that has numerous pitfalls and sensitivities. Unfortunately, there is a general misconception that if a student is showing vocal limitation, then that's the way it is and not much can be done about it. But in the same way that water is naturally clean and clear until it is muddied by some kind of external matter, so is a sound vibration *pure* and *unadulterated* until it has been constricted or released by the energetic state of the human instrument. All too often I hear finite statements like, "I have no range, I have a breathy tonal quality, I sing out of tune, my support doesn't work, I can't project my voice and there is a big break between my registers," which, put more constructively, should be, "*Why* do I appear to have a limited range, *what* is contributing to the airiness in my tonal quality, *how* do I maintain my pitch throughout a phrase and *what* do I need to do to blend the registers more effectively?"

"Don't look where you fall, but where you slipped"
- African proverb

Something has to happen (*cause*) for an action to occur (*effect or result*), so since we are all born with the ability to breathe, project, support and engage sound, there has to be a reason for any compromise or dysfunction in these areas. All too often, singers become fixated on the *collision site* and set about trying to fix a problem that is symptomatic of an earlier vocal miscalculation. Although there is a general perception that technique is something to be *added* to the voice, it is in fact, developing the ability to prevent a mishap or collision from happening by avoiding the cause.

Let's take a train wreck, for example. Imagine a derailed train that has collided with a concrete pylon. Now rewind to a few seconds before the collision and you will see the exact *cause* of the derailment. Be it a faulty signal, debris on the tracks, or an error of the driver, the collision was a symptom or result of any or all of these causes.

In singing, one such collision is commonly known as a vocal *crack* or *break*, which at one time or another singers both male and female will have to learn to negotiate. This can occur while engaging the head voice, the chest voice, or when crossing from one register to another, but it is important to understand that this is only a symptom of interrupted *vocal* alignment or placement, and can easily be rectified with the right technical information and ongoing practice. The same issue arises with the endless struggle many singers have with high notes. By and large we are conditioned by the shapes, colours, and textures we see in the external world, which are directly, or indirectly responsible for our perception, experiences, and subsequent reality. For example, when we look at a keyboard or manuscript with printed notation we see *distance,* or what we refer to as *intervals*. These are merely structures created for playing and reading music and not at all indicative of the real distance between notes. This perception wrongly encourages singers to lift and strain their necks to access high notes and to dig or compress to reach the low. However, it must be understood that this distance is an illusion and therefore cannot be measured, so the vocal *result* is your only true guide.

> **"If you don't know where you're going, you will probably end up somewhere else."**
> *- Lawrence J. Peter*

When I first began working with Tania she was a bright, vivacious, but vocally raw 19 old with her heart set on a career in musical theatre. Before we had even begun the lesson, she looked at me with tears in her eyes and said, "I hate my voice!" I asked her to sing me a scale and after only a few notes I could hear that Tania was facing the same technical challenges as most other singers. The lower chest notes were solid and clear but as she went higher they became weighted and harsh making a clear transition into the head voice impossible. The next few notes disappeared altogether only to reappear as a weak and breathy head tone that was obviously difficult to sustain and only capable of accessing a fraction of her natural female range. A similar scenario happened on the descending notes, which became virtually inaudible, only to magically manifest into the solid, clear chest quality she had begun with. "My voice is possessed!" she cried. I laughed and told her that she had simply fallen prey to the dreaded *crocodile pit.*" The look on her face told me that she had no clue what I meant, so I explained to her that I was describing the naturally occurring *fault lines* or weaker passages of the voice and went on to explain that if these passages were not negotiated properly they would instantly became a technical *falling deck of cards*, giving the singer an unrealistically negative impression of his or her vocal ability.

However, before I could begin to give Tania the necessary technical exercises, I needed to put certain things into perspective for her. I asked her if the earlier statement she had made about hating her voice was true, only to find that she in fact loved to sing in her chest voice but had never done any work on the upper register. This was largely due to the fact that she had been singing in a rock band and the repertoire she had been doing did not require her to use her head voice and if it had, she would simply change the key. "Do you understand that if you have only ever used one register, your voice will most surely be imbalanced?" I asked. "And if you have not used your head voice before, isn't it natural that it would be underdeveloped and weak?" She nodded as I went on to explain that one of the quickest ways to create a break in the registers is to consistently change from head to chest in exactly the same place. Tania did not understand the reason for this so I used the analogy of *bush bashing*, which is an Australian colloquialism for creating a new pathway in the bush by walking the same way dozens of times. Eventually, nothing much grows in that place as the human traffic is constantly destroying the new plants, which eventually renders the ground barren and infertile.

She was now beginning to understand that there were valid reasons and explanations behind the difficulties she was experiencing, and was now in the right frame of mind to explore some vocal options. I went on to explain that every skill known to humans relies on *balance* and, in the context of singing, balance can also be known as *placement*. Placement serves to align notes and registers into a position that allows them to flow seamlessly from one to the other, resulting in uninterrupted vocal flow. Ideally, to access this point of balance – or placement - the voice must be animated and resonating in the mask - or frontal cavities - of the face, but the difficulty lies in the fact that the singing apparatus is housed inside the body and can only be understood if and when the correct vocal sensations have been experienced enough times to become an integrated awareness. When we sing, a complex and fascinating process of autosuggestion is at play, where *thought* is being converted to *sound*, and *sound* is being converted into the *action* of singing. Action is *manifested thought*, but we cannot create a thought about something we have not yet experienced. So we must firstly understand the feeling of the action and then the associated physical result, and it is the memory of this feeling that eventually allows us to recreate it at will.

I continued by asking her to sing a five note ascending and descending scale several times and, each time we began a new scale, I asked her to change registers on a different note. For example, I asked her to sing the first four notes in chest and the fifth in head, then the first three notes in chest and the last two in head until she was singing only the first note in chest voice and the last four in head voice. The result was much improved after a few attempts and this simple change had noticeably influenced the coordination of several other technical components. Choosing to change registers in a different place forced Tania to lessen the air pressure, making the transition much smoother. This, in turn, influenced the way she prepared the breath and onset the sound, which kept her voice grounded and the tonal quality intact. I then asked her to think of the five notes as one continuous phrase and to play the game of *follow the leader*, where each note was responsible for setting up the success of the next one, irrespective of the register she was using. I also asked her to become aware of any note becoming unstable and to do whatever she intuitively felt she needed to do to stabilise it.

Tania became very excited as she began to understand that when there was a disconnection between the registers, it was caused by the way she had set up the notes before it and that she could actually sense it before it occurred if she tuned into the vocal sensations. Over the next three years we worked solidly and consistently on these areas, after which time she had not only managed to access all of her soprano range, but the difference between the registers was almost imperceptible.

"Learning to sing is unlearning the barriers that prevent free flowing sound"
- A Colliver

Sound is a *continuum,* as are water and air, and as their very nature is *flow*, they cannot be severed, broken or lost. They can however, be interrupted or blocked. As we generally experience the world in a finite and external way, the conscious mind finds the surrender to this flow hard to comprehend, and a struggle begins between the analytical mind and the requirements of organic action. If sound is indeed symptomatic of the human condition, and we are largely unaware of what we do and how we do it, the challenge is to become more conscious of how our thoughts are motivating our actions. Breath control, support, placement, range, tone, volume, and projection are all organised by the required vocal result, so as it is not possible to measure this intellectually, they must be allowed to organise and coordinate themselves. This, in essence, asks for the act of singing to become a *waking meditation,* whereby the *inner eye* or *intuition* is trained to become aware of the experience it is having and to make creative decisions based on the physical sensations - rather than on conceptual knowledge.

When we look *out* at the physical world, most of us believe that what we are seeing is the complete picture but, in fact, there is so much more behind, beyond, and within what we are seeing externally that it can only be fully understood if it is observed with the wisdom of the *inner eye*. When this *meditation* or *inner focus* is used in relationship to singing, we are not so much withdrawing our attention from the outside world, as is the case in other meditational practices but, rather, we are observing and negotiating our voices from within. This is not easy, as releasing attachment to what we see and hear brings on a feeling of physical and emotional *free fall*, but eventually we will find ourselves becoming more sensitive to the way we energize sound, and will allow ourselves to *be sung* rather than allowing ourselves to be *doing* the singing. This is not as mysterious as it sounds, but it does require patience, consistency, focus, and practice if it is to be achieved. The choice to adopt this approach, however, is made easier if we understand that this is the only way to reliable vocal control.

Exercises:

a) *Look for any resistance you might have to exploring vocal options and gently begin to let them go by understanding that experimentation can, in fact, be enjoyable and fun.*

b) *Feel where the weaker passages of your voice begin and end, and work calmly, intelligently, and joyfully towards strengthening and understanding them with the knowledge that this is part of the journey towards vocal stability and control.*

c) *Become aware of the way you warm up your voice. If you regularly use the same scales and vowel sounds, begin to vary or change them.*

d) *Extend your vocal range in both registers, firstly with an increase of one semitone and then one tone when you feel ready to do so.*

e) *Play with the resonating qualities in both registers by purposely creating a constricted sound, a nasal sound, a swallowed sound, a disconnected sound, a pressed sound, a cracked or broken sound, and an ugly sound, and then aim for a sound that feels beautiful, connected, and free.*

f) *Record yourself and constructively listen back to what you have done and then decide if you achieved the result you wanted. If not, assess how close you were and try again.*

g) *Practice register changing exercises (women, chest to head and male, chest to falsetto), e.g., octave jumps, intervals of fifths, or a simple five-note scale ascending and descending.*

h) *Record yourself doing this to see if you can detect where the notes begin to fall into the break and then go back and try again by tuning into the feeling of the sound as it is occurring.*

i) *Regularly write down any questions you may have and seek out the answers via the Internet, books, or your vocal mentor.*

7

BUILD ON THE ROCK
Foundations Make the House

"Discipline is the bridge between goals and accomplishment"
- Jim Rohn

There are many schools of thought on how to achieve great singing, but although most will agree on what is considered to be a wonderful vocal result, the methodologies used to achieve them are diverse and arguable. What is, however, undeniable is that certain principles allow certain results. On my first teaching day at an arts school in Singapore, the Musical Theatre students were given an opportunity to introduce themselves to the staff members and to one another. I distinctly remember the moment a handsome young man stood up and said, "Hi, my name is Bernd. I'm Australian and I come from the *dark side*," only to be interrupted by a striking beauty named Ashleigh, who jumped to her feet, rolled her eyes and cried out in mock despair, "I'm from the *dark side* too!" Laughter abounded when it was discovered that the dark side was, in fact, classical training and although it was said in jest, in truth these students appeared to be apologising for the fact that they had a solid vocal background. Why they felt the need to apologise was an intriguing question for me.

Depending on what you read, and the experience of those you question, there will be a diversity of answers and opinions on the subject of classical training and its value. As with most things, ignorance, dogma, and elitist attitudes have the ability to veil and taint the intrinsic nature of the classic art forms, encouraging those less well-versed on the subject to "throw out the baby with the bathwater." Stability, endurance, refinement, simplicity, harmony, and elegance are the classical elements ballet brings to dance, Shakespeare brings to acting, yoga brings to sport, and opera brings to singing. Most, if not all, of my teaching focuses on the *re-stumping* of a student's technique. In Australia, re-stumping is known as the replacement of the rotting or defective stumps, which cause structural damage to a house by compromising its stability and balance. Similar to this, the classical principles create a kind of foundational *scaffolding,* giving the singer a reliable platform on which to play. I often quote the analogy of a wild stallion where the horse has energy and fire but is magnificently wild and undirected. A good horse breaker creates boundaries for the animal without stifling its spirit, allowing freedom and expression. This, too, should apply to all singers - but classical training can only be useful if a teacher understands its relationship to styles other than operatic, and helps the singer understand its benefits and relevance to the genres he or she is exploring.

One glaring misconception among most singers is that classical training is opera, but in truth it only *allows* you the option of moving into this style by developing the necessary technical control to coordinate language, style, tone, range, flexibility, and the stamina to project sound without artificial amplification. Although I believe the demands of operatic training to be the best way to access the complete potential of the human instrument, it is the elitist opinion that other styles of music are inferior that ostracises those not wishing to train as classical singers. This is ill-informed, unnecessary, and, in my opinion, the reason this kind of training is so often overlooked in the education of contemporary singers. Despite genre and style of music, the human instrument balances itself in the same way and therefore the foundational training principles should be the same for all voices. Air still needs to enter the lungs and pass over the vocal folds, support still needs to be engaged, vocal control is still paramount in achieving pitch, range, projection, and communication and, although the stylistic language differs, this will naturally organise itself when and if the genre is approached correctly.

In the area of musical theatre we find styles ranging from operatic through to rock, requiring a greater range of stylistic versatility than any other musical genre. And, although the singer might be extremely accomplished in contemporary styles, unless he or she has an integrated classical foundation, works like *The Phantom of the Opera*, *West Side Story*, *My Fair Lady*, *Candide,* and *Porgy and Bess*, that demand what is known as *legitimate singing*, are all but impossible to execute. I'm certain that operatic exercises are paramount for ongoing vocal maintenance, particularly in the course of a long running show or regular singing, as the nature of the rounded vowels prevents the muscles from settling into the contemporary shapes of speech, which so easily result in lowered placement and the shortening of range.

Good Vibrations
Kelly was performing the leading role of Scaramouche in an international production of *We Will Rock You* and I was more than surprised when she called me asking for a vocal session as I had seen the show the evening before, and thought hers to be a stand out performance. She told me that she wasn't really having vocal problems as such, but that her voice was feeling *tight* and not flowing as easy as it should. The role she was playing sat predominantly in the chest register requiring a lot of belting and rock nuances. I asked her to demonstrate how she was warming up her voice before the show, and after listening to a few scales knew exactly what the problem was. I remembered several conversations I'd had with dancers who complained that although they were performing every night, their bodies were becoming less flexible and they had lost some of their previous form. This, they explained, was because the demands of the show they were in were only using part of their overall skill, and so taking extra dance classes, usually ballet, outside of the show was imperative for them to stay in shape. Kelly was warming up in the style she was singing in the show without using any vibrato or head voice and, over time, this had begun to tighten and limit her range.

I find the word *vibrato* to be sadly misunderstood and misaligned due to the many compromised ways in which it can manifest. However, it is undeniably the result of an open throat and healthy closure of the vocal cords imperative to vocal freedom. I instructed Kelly to create vibrato on every note in the scale, whether she was in chest voice or head voice, to release the vocal shapes she was using from contemporary to operatic. This slowly began to awaken the natural principles of support, release, and projection, and after an hour she left somewhat bemused but vocally released and intellectually inspired. The next day she called me with excitement and disbelief at the ease with which she had sung that night and was now adopting the same warm up technique we had done in the session as part of her daily routine.

Faking it
David was a twenty three year old Australian who was recording his first original album, but the process was being hampered by the fact that he was ending up vocally fatigued at the end of every session and needing to take several days off to recover enough to continue. I explained to him that the fatigue he was experiencing was due to the jaw tension and constriction he was using to produce a rock sound and that I was going to use operatic exercises to help his voice so the abdominal muscles could begin to support the sound rather than his throat. David looked apprehensive and lamented, "I really do want to sing better, but I don't want to sound like Pavarotti." "Don't worry, I'm not asking you to sing your rock songs operatically," I said, "but you will begin to see how these exercises will

profoundly influence the overall result by giving you more vocal freedom and consistency." I went on to help him understand that opera to the voice was the same as yoga to the body, in the way that both served not only to release and lengthen muscles but were also vital for ongoing maintenance and health.

I could see that this parallel made sense to him, so he reluctantly signed up for his first hour of vocal *boot camp*. Being Australian and a rock singer, it was inevitable that his vowel sounds would be full of diphthongs and the legato line throughout the vocal phrases would be virtually non-existent. "What's a diphthong?" he asked. I explained that it was the occurrence of two vowel sounds happening within the same syllable, like *day, how, why,* and *new*, but that he had to learn to sing with the Italian vowels of *A, E, I, O* and *U* if they were to sound remotely classical. After several self-conscious attempts, he seemed somewhat disheartened and unsure if this would be the answer to his problems. I explained that no one is born singing this way and because it isn't *natural,* we firstly have to fake it or pretend to be an opera singer until we become familiar with the unusual sensations and our bodies become comfortable with the *posture*. For weeks, David thrashed about like a fish out of water as he struggled with the foreign sensations of the rounded vowels and the embarrassment of emulating a style he disliked intensely, but outside of his lessons he was experiencing marked vocal improvement in the recording sessions and much less fatigue. Months later he proudly placed a newly released CD in my hands and waited anxiously as I listened to the first two tracks. "Wow, you really sound great," I said, "but there's no sign of Pavarotti?" He laughed and understood my reference to his initial fear of sounding classical in his songs, and explained that he was now convinced of the importance of the work we had done together and would continue working the same way on his own. David has gone on to enjoy a very successful career as a singer/songwriter, not only more technically aware and confident but, most importantly, free of vocal fatigue.

Classical training need not ostracise or intimidate, but should be seen as a necessary enhancement and stabiliser for the physical and intellectual requirements of solid and reliable vocal technique. Misrepresentation and misunderstanding of the style should not deter singers from its true and essential substance, which - if used intelligently - simply serves as a *means to an end* for all styles and genres.

8
THE GRAND CANYON
Crossing in Style

"Versatility is the product of an open mind."
- Anonymous

"**Curiosity killed the cat**" is, according to the *trusty* Wikipedia, a proverb used to warn of the dangers of unnecessary investigation or experimentation. And, although the words "God fashioned hell for the inquisitive," by Saint Augustine in 397AD, and "He that pryeth into every cloud may be struck with a thunderbolt," by John Clarke in 1639, reveal that this attitude has been around for centuries, I personally, cannot find a justifiable reason as to why.

Avoiding danger is one thing but avoiding knowledge is quite another, and I can only surmise that one's curiosity has a tendency to reveal another's ignorance, which can be threatening to the safety of the individual and the status quo. Or perhaps we don't even know that we are being unadventurous and one-dimensional, which would explain why so many singers are reticent to explore more than one vocal style. Too many times I have heard singers vocally classify themselves, only to hear them sing in what must be described as some kind of *hybrid* musical style belonging nowhere in particular. All the *eggs*, so to speak, have been put in one basket, blurring the lines of the very characteristics that make the styles unique. For many, near enough is good enough, which only serves to create an air of mediocrity where there could be excellence. The only area exempt from this confusion is opera, as the purist nature and technical demands of it cannot be executed without the correct vocal approach. However, there has been more than one opera singer who has recorded a *crossover* album without any comprehension of styles other than classical. Singing a pop song with the vocal production of an opera singer may be fine in itself, but to believe that it actually works or is right for the genre is misguided and misleading.

Opera, classical, musical theatre, pop, jazz, and rock are all unique and separate musical languages in themselves and, although, some styles are close enough to each other to be fused into crossover styles, others are not. Although fundamental principles will apply to every art form, the demands of each style will organise these principles into any number of creative outcomes. No one wears all styles of clothing at the same time, or eats all kinds of food in one sitting. Neither will one attempt boxing while doing yoga, or try speaking English, French, and Russian all at the same time. Opera demands melodrama, technical precision, stamina, and the ability to project the voice acoustically, whereas contemporary styles will ask for the peeling back, bending, or breaking of these rules, placing less emphasis on vocal perfection and more on organic communication. This, in turn, will inform the overall vocal posture and automatically modify the language of the style. When I speak of vocal *posture*, I am not only referring to the physical attitude needed to inhabit each style, but also to the vocal registers partial to that particular type of music. Inhabiting different styles, however, is no easy feat, as musical language has to be experienced to be understood and many of us are extremely limited when it comes to stylistic exposure.

Much of my work has been with performers from the broad genre of musical theatre. Gone are the days when a singer can *beg* vocal limitation and expect to enjoy ongoing employment, and many times there are singers who miss opportunities for this very reason.

Maree had just finished playing the role of Christine in the Australian production of *The Phantom of the Opera* and was now in the running for the part of Grizabella in *Cats*. For those of you who are not familiar with these two roles, they are diametrically opposed in style and could not be more different in their vocal demands. Christine is written for a light soprano with colouratura abilities, and Grizabella for a contemporary singer with the ability to belt a top Db. In my opinion, Maree's voice was much more suited to classical repertoire but as she was also able to sing convincingly in her chest voice, she was being considered for one of the most prestigious and coveted roles in musical theatre history. There was only one problem; Maree believed she could get away with using a strong contemporary head voice in the climax of the song Memory, and although she could blend both the registers together extremely well, it was not the vocal quality the musical director wanted. After a phone call from him informing me that if she could stay in her chest register and *belt* the required notes the role was hers, we promptly set about working on accessing this part of her voice. It was a *crash course* in this style of singing for Maree, but it's wonderfully rewarding to see a singer's capabilities come to the fore when given no choice. Happily she won the part and is now more versatile and bankable because of it.

Although fascinating, helping a student understand the basic differences from one style to another is challenging due to fact that they all possess a different *feel* or *groove*, and this *feel* can only be understood through direct experience of the style itself, which is difficult if a singer's musical influence is limited or biased. Those most adept and open to embracing more than one style are generally from a culture that is steeped in musical history. For example, the music of the United States reflects its multi-ethnic population through the colourful styles of hip hop, blues, country, gospel, jazz, pop, techno, barbershop, rock 'n' roll, folk, musical theatre, and opera, and boasts many of the greatest singers in the world. On the other hand, there are countries where music is not the *pulse* of society, so the cultural affinity with and approach to rhythm, colour, and movement is often cerebral or ambivalent. On many occasions I have been confused when students have informed me that they have studied what they call a *pop technique*, only to find out that they have merely sung pop songs or learned from a teacher who is a contemporary singer. Equally confusing is a student claiming to have studied classically, who is in actuality someone who has not been exposed to contemporary music or, in the case of females, have only sung in their head register. In the same way, a statement like "My name is Tom, I'm a tenor and I'm going to sing 'Maggie May' by Rod Stewart," is incongruous, in that the term *tenor* is an operatic classification and yet Tom is auditioning with a pop song. Although this may seem trivial or unimportant to the panel, from an artistic point of view the singer is revealing a lack of clarity and knowledge, which cannot help but influence the standard of his or her performing ability.

Jack of all trades
RJ was thirty years old, physically stunning, and a celebrity in the Philippines, which explained the charming arrogance he exuded as he swept into my studio for the first time. This arrogance, I was to find, veiled a deep insecurity about his talent, musical intelligence, and theatrical future, and I had no inkling of the journey we would take together over the next seven years. RJ was at a crossroads in his career as he was being told in auditions that he was too classical for the contemporary roles and not classical enough for the *legitimate*. The way he had been singing was no longer giving him the acclaim he was used to, and he felt he was being left behind in an industry where the emphasis had shifted away from *middle of the road* and more towards *cutting edge*. Despite his natural vocal talent and undeniable personal charisma, the way he sang reminded me of a good Karaoke singer who was

stuck in the *club crooner* style of the eighties, and although he had said that he sang jazz, pop, and musical theatre, it soon became obvious to me that he sang everything in this laidback manner. The lower parts of his voice had the warmth of a classical baritone, but as he moved to the extremities of his range the quality became *thinner* and more contemporary in style, giving the impression of multiple voices. Apart from the fact that he was unknowingly blurring the lines among several styles, his voice reminded me of a pot-bound plant, in the way that a plant can exist in a small pot but does not flourish the way it would if given new soil and a larger pot to accommodate the growing root system. In the same way, his voice had reach a place where it could no longer grow within the confines of its *playground* and he needed to become aware of the stylistic choices he was or wasn't making to allow his voice more definition and freedom. I told him that as with many untrained but gifted singers, what works for them initially tends to reach a plateau, and although they may excel in a particular style, exploring the finer details of other vocal styles could only contribute to the broadminded intelligence particular to those most likely to succeed.

The greatest challenge for RJ was going to be changing his somewhat complacent approach to musical repertoire, and my challenge was going to be articulating the fundamental principles that constitute a style. As with all art forms, tangible, physical action always makes much more sense to a student than conceptual discussion, so I needed to demonstrate some of the differences before going any further. I sang the first few bars of Gounod's *Ave Maria* operatically and then changed to a pop version of Cindy Lauper's *Girls Just Wanna Have Fun*. I then sang a classical version of *Summertime,* a jazz rendition of *Can't Help Lovin' That Man*, and ended with a chorus from the rock song *Black Velvet*. He seemed confused that my operatic voice was completely different to my contemporary sound, so I asked him whether he spoke other languages, to which he answered yes. "When you speak English, does it feel and sound the same as Tagalog?" I asked. "No," he answered, beginning to understand what I was getting at. "And would you say that the shapes in your mouth are organising themselves differently depending on which language you are speaking?" He nodded and began to realise that I was likening vocal styles to different languages, and there were inherent differences in them all. "However," I added, "You can be speaking English coloured with the accent of Tagalog, which will compromise the authenticity of both languages, and this, I believe, is what you are doing with your vocal styles."

A matter of degree

As with all of my students, my mission with RJ was to help him understand that because there are so many vocal options from which to choose, it is imperative that singers know what choices they are making, and why. Although there is more than the potential for confusion in the analysis of the differences, to make sense of them meant I needed to venture into the complex *recipe* of sound itself.

Every sound vibration consists of the frequencies known as *lows, mids,* and *highs* or, as referred to in the arena of singing, *sob, speech, and twang.* The low frequencies or *sob,* make the sound dark, powerful, and warm, allowing the voice buoyancy and *float*. The midrange frequencies, or *speech*, give the sound its energy and communication ability. And the high or *twang* frequencies give a sound its presence, shine, and lifelike quality. By modifying or highlighting any one of these components, the sound will organise itself into any number of different combinations, creating its own particular personality or style.

Operatic quality is a complex mixture of *speech, twang,* and *sob*, with a large emphasis on *sob*, which is imperative for maximum resonation and acoustic projection. *Vibrato* is a direct result of this component and a non-negotiable feature of this style and, in turn, has a direct impact on how the vowels and consonants are modified. However, if this is not balanced correctly, the language becomes indecipherable and the tonal quality, energy, and brightness are compromised. In the *classical* arena of lieder, art song, sacred music, and *legitimate* musical theatre, the vocal requirements are the same, but there is either less or none of the operatic melodrama which tempers the degree to which vibrato occurs, thus changing the overall vocal effect. This applies to both male and female voices, although women must predominantly use head register for classical and operatic repertoire.

In the eclectic arena of pop, rock, jazz, blues, and folk music, the differences sit more in *feel*, *groove*, and musical interpretation, than in the core vocal components present in the sound. Operatic *sob* generally has no place within these styles, with the exception of the bass baritones of country music and the theatrics of alternative performers like Kate Bush, Björk, and Lena Lovich. These styles demand the bending or breaking of the classical rules, preferring rhythmic and melodic improvisations, lazy diction, and vocal imperfections, and it is from this that the twang of country, the croon of jazz, the gravel and rasp of a rock 'n' roll, the husky tones of the blues and the melancholic lilt of folk tunes are born.

Belting can be done in any register and in any style other than opera and, when done correctly, highlights the twang frequency, fueling the heightened energies of passion, joy, and excitement. However, it is how a singer inhabits a style that allows its authenticity and freedom to shine, as anyone can put on a designer gown, suit, mini skirt, or jeans, but only a few will wear them as they were meant to be worn.

When exploring other genres with students, it is most constructive to begin with one close to the style they are well versed in. For example, when introducing a pop singer to musical theatre, I begin with the contemporary shows first and gradually move towards those more classical. In the same way, a classical singer will benefit more from exploring music close to the style he or she is used to, rather than jumping into the diametrically opposed language of jazz, pop, or rock. However, it is important to note that exploring styles and their differences does not mean there is an expectation that a singer will relate to, or master them all. This is generally not possible and in most cases would be counter-productive as we all possess different vocal strengths and musical affinities. On the other hand, possessing a library of vocal choices not only allows a singer to be more articulate with his or her own style, but also provides a more extensive understanding of the multidimensional craft of singing.

RJ was offered the role of Thuy in *Miss Saigon* on the proviso that he worked regularly with me to ensure he would not vocally fatigue under the strain of a role that had the tessitura suited to a classical tenor. This was timely and well deserved as we had spent the last few years stabilising his technique and he was now a much more sophisticated and articulate performer. He continued to work on his voice with renewed vigor and confidence, and transformed into one of the most pro-active, intelligent, and interesting students I have ever worked with. We now had technical discussions about everything from vocal maintenance to the stylistic choices he was making which, in time, allowed him to become a very different calibre of performer.

The best way to learn a language, be it spoken or sung, is to submerge yourself in it's ambience, rhythm, and energy. Fear of the unknown only serves to limit possibilities and, as we must *imitate* before we *assimilate*, we have to expect inauthentic moments and disjointed execution of unfamiliar action or skill before we can hope to experience anything close to mastery. However, if it is not possible to absorb culturally, there are many other ways to explore and experiment with sound and styles - but the real integration happens with regular execution of these styles.

Explore the following sounds and qualities of *opera, twang, sob, falsetto,* and *speech,* analysing the resonating sensations of the shapes within your face and body.

- **Twang** (ugly, nasal, thin, constricted, harsh)

- **Sob** (hollow, round, warm, swallowed)

- **Falsetto** (breathy, disconnected, weak)

- **Incorrect Speech** (forced, pressed, constricted, rasping)

- **Correct Speech** (bright, grounded, forward, released, belted)

Questions:

1. *Which sounds feel open and expansive, what feels limited and constricted, what feels unfamiliar and unsafe, what feels uncomfortable and silly, what feels exciting and unexplored?*

2. *Are there other styles I wish to explore and if so, why don't I try?*

3. *Which style suits me the best and how many others realistically lie within my vocal capacity?*

Experiment:

a) *Make up your own sentences and say the words with some of the above sounds.*

b) *Make up your own tunes and sing them in the same way.*

  c) *Listen to and observe the styles that appeal to you.*

  d) *Try to imitate one of them.*

  e) *Record or video yourself and view your efforts constructively.*

  f) *Observe whether you are feeling self conscious or uncomfortable with the process and try to approach everything with a sense of humor and an open mind.*

Execute:

  a) *Classify the style you sing and research this more thoroughly to see if you are authentically within its framework. If not, work towards becoming more specific and articulate.*

  b) *Choose several different pieces that sit within your genre of music, e.g., classical (opera, operetta, lieder, art song, oratorio, sacred) or musical theatre (classical/legit, jazz, pop, rock). Research the differences and execute them to the best of your ability.*

"Attitude is a little thing that makes a big difference."
- Winston Churchill

  For many years, becoming a versatile artist was an exciting but elusive idea to me, and I can still remember how long it took to let go of the classical *safety net* I had always relied on. When I did, the results were informative, surprising, and quite exhilarating. I had often heard myself utter the inane words, "I don't sing in my spare time," as I considered myself to be a professional opera singer who sang on a stage and not impromptu at social events. But the truth was that I didn't know how to drop my operatic *identity* and allow my voice to express itself in other styles or registers. I secretly envied those who sat around the proverbial *camp fire,* sharing themselves spontaneously and imperfectly, and I desperately wanted the same kind of freedom for myself. Not everybody does, or should, and although I still believe my forte to be in classical singing, it is important to me to practice what I teach and to discover dimensions of creativity within myself that run deeper than mere technical skill. I have a four-wheel drive car but have never gone four-wheel driving. I play a top of the range midi keyboard every day, but have never seriously explored the midi section. I have a Mac computer and iPhone that are sorely underutilised, and I sang every day for 25 years and only used a part of my voice. However, it doesn't really matter what we do with what we have, as long as we know that there are any number of options and opportunities waiting to be explored and taken, if and when we are ready. These options and opportunities may not only serve to provide many of the answers we seek, but will also allow a more informed and broadminded approach towards the world, each other, and ourselves.

NOTES:

9
LOST IN TRANSLATION
The Language Barrier

"If you talk to a man in a language he understands, it goes to his head. If you talk to him in his own language, it goes to his heart."
- Nelson Mandela

I grew up with two extremely articulate parents. My father a speech therapist and school teacher, and my mother an educator with TAA Airlines, a self-taught naturopath, and poet. My family did not own a television for the first eight years of my life, so instead we sat enthralled at the feet of my father as he read chapter after chapter from the novels of Charles Dickens, Mark Twain, and Lewis Carroll. My mother spoke extremely well due to several years abroad, and took immense pride in the fact that all her children were intelligent, had a comprehensive vocabulary and an excellent command of the English language. As a child I was an avid reader and would visit the characters in my books whenever I had a spare moment. I loved going on adventures with the *Famous Five*, wandering the fields of *Narnia*, and attending tea parties with Alice and the Mad Hatter, and could literally *hear*, *taste,* and *feel* these people and places. I would learn my favorite books off by heart and describe the colourful images I had stored away in my mind to anyone who would listen. But most unexpected for me has been the realisation that the passion and interest I have for the work I do does not come from my love of music but, rather, from the fascination I have for translating *concept* into *language* and *language* into *tangible physical experience.*

The sublime to the ridiculous

Although a powerful tool, language can never *be* the experience it is trying to describe, and therefore it is vital that the concept behind the action of singing becomes tangible, or *real,* to each individual. Only then can vocal education be effective and constructive. Many a student has come to work with me claiming to have had several years training, only to find out that few if any of the technical fundamentals are in place, and when asked to explain his or her understanding of words like *placement, support,* and *resonance,* most are unable to articulate it clearly. To describe something, one must have a word that embraces it, and to have a word that embraces something means it must make logical sense to the individual.

Singing is a little like operating in the dark, as the vocal mechanism cannot be seen, and therefore the language used to describe its intricacies can at best only be analytical and conceptual. This fact encourages vocal teachers to use words like "kind of…, sort of…, a bit like…, try thinking of a…, imagine how you would…", inciting many sublime and ridiculous anecdotes or analogies in the hope of explaining the unexplainable. "Think of your buttocks on your hard palate," "sing the sound between the notes," "pretend your head is hollow," "breathe into your feet," "imagine you're standing on glass in stilettos," " be someone else," "take a running jump," "imagine you have two chopsticks up your nostrils," "suck up spaghetti," "pretend you're giving birth," are just a few of the innovative visualisations used in the hope of achieving technical precision and control. Can they work? Absolutely. Do they work? Not always, as words at the best of times are overflowing with ambiguities and ill-defined concepts which, in my opinion, are the source of most, if not all of the vocal confusion in the world today.

One man's meat is another man's poison

There is a plethora of words and terminology being used to encourage and assist students in their quest to achieve correct vocal results, but we all interpret and respond to words differently and therefore what might be effective for one student does not necessarily work for another. I was extremely lucky to have studied under several fine teachers over the years and credit much of my technical knowledge to them. Singing teachers would work with me on the intricacies of vocal technique, and vocal coaches on repertoire and languages. All of them seemed to be united in their vocal vision for me but the analogies, concepts, ideologies, and language they used to convey them were varied and diverse. Interestingly, I don't remember experiencing any difficulty interpreting what each teacher meant, which may have been due to the fact that I was a singing teacher myself and familiar with the numerous ways in which one could describe things.

One winter's afternoon in Ballarat, I found myself competing against Jane at an Eisteddfod and was immediately taken with her rich and effortless soprano voice. She was 21, married, with her heart set on having a large family and living on a farm somewhere out of the city. Singing, for Jane, had been what you might call an after-thought, and the interest being shown in her talent was daunting but extremely exciting for her. As we talked further, I discovered that she had just begun to study with Thomas, who was also my own beloved teacher. Thomas' approach to vocal technique was more pedagogical and physiological than it was organic or intuitive and Jane would often put herself down for her inability to understand much of the information he was imparting. A few months later I watched her perform again but this time she seemed unusually tentative and restrained, almost as though she had lost her nerve, and I was surprised to see her struggling with musical passages that had appeared effortless in the past. I felt her approach had become somewhat technical and *worked*, and later, when she lamented that the more she learned the more complicated singing became, I knew that a process that had been simple and natural for her had become complex and inorganic. I suggested that she go back to what she had been doing several months before and not to worry if the language she used to access these results was not the same as the one Thomas might use, as it was only the outcome that was important. I cannot say whether the language being used by the teacher was a contributing factor to Jane's confusion or not, but there is always the danger that in an effort to describe an experience with words, natural actions can become so overly analysed that they simply become "lost in translation."

There are many things in life that language has a hard time describing and, more often than not, the words we use have several meanings or interpretations. Therefore it is important to keep an eye on how a student is processing the information being given, and to modify or change it accordingly. Personally, I believe if you understand the subject matter being discussed there will always be a way to communicate anything to anyone, so if a student is confused or non-responsive to your language, another way of delivering the message can most certainly be found.

The contexts in which common vocal terminology like *pitch, support, placement, resonance, energy, space, vibrato,* and *expression* is used are wide and varied and too numerous to mention. But somewhere in this myriad of choices, there will be one that *turns on the light* or *makes the penny drop* for a singer, after which a new level of vocal integration can begin. For example:

- **Pitch** - *in tune, intonation, phonation, "in the pocket"*

- **Support** - *anchored, grounded, earthed, connected, balanced, aligned*

- **Placement** - *positioning, up, hooked in, forward, in the mask, height, nasality, twang*

- **Resonance** - *quality, tone, substance, core, timbre, colour, richness, fullness, sonorous, ringing, clarity*

- **Energy** - *movement, vigor, oomph, vitality, momentum, float, flow, power, strength, intensity, implosion, explosion, freedom, life-force, pressure, force, push, weight, juice, attack, drive*

- **Space** - *open, round, hollow, column, pathway, corridor, yawn, sob, release, back*

- **Vibrato** - *spin, reverberation, tremolo, life, buoyancy, shimmer, dimension*

- **Expression** - *personality, animation, attitude, authenticity, articulation, individuality, sass, chutzpa*

For a teacher to choose and use language effectively, he or she needs to have the ability to tune in or *read* another, which can only be done through observation and empathy. However, it is important to understand that the responsibility of language does not lie only with a teacher, but also with you, the student. If you do not understand your teacher's language, tell him or her so that they know how you feel, and try to be specific about what it is that is confusing you. If your teacher cannot demonstrate or articulate how you can achieve the required singing results, perhaps you should look for help elsewhere.

Language will only ever be able to describe the *action* of singing, but it can never be the *experience* of singing itself. Many a vocal casualty occurs when singers becomes stuck in the *birthing canal* between concept and action. So if you find yourself in this position, try to forget the words, go to the action of singing, and work your way backwards to how you personally describe the sensations of what you are doing. Your voice needs clear messages to coordinate itself at optimum level, and clear messages can only be formed with knowledge and understanding of the required outcome. You are the master of your ship and therefore must find your own language for your own vocal voyage.

Questions:

1. *Do you possess a broad vocabulary?*

2. *If you don't understand something, do you feel that it must be your fault?*

3. *Do you ask questions when you are confused about something?*

4. *If given a sentence, could you say it in several different ways?*

5. *Are you articulate and clear when you describe things?*

6. *Do you understand the words you are using?*

7. *Do you know how to listen and are you observant and empathetic towards others?*

Exercises:

a) *When you speak, contemplate the language you are using and whether or not you are being clear and concise in what you are saying.*

b) *Expand your vocabulary by learning several new words a week and begin using them in your daily conversations.*

c) *Become aware of how many times you do not ask a question for fear of appearing unintelligent or inflammatory.*

d) *Observe whether you listen to what people are saying or are simply waiting to speak.*

e) *When you do not understand what someone is saying to you, try asking them to explain it in another way.*

f) *Take a word and research how many other ways this word can be said.*

g) *Try to articulate your own vocal methodology to see if you do indeed understand how to access the results you want.*

NOTES:

10

CHILD'S PLAY
Out of the Mouths of Babes

"A child is not a vase to be filled, but a fire to be lit."
- Francois Rabelais

Children have a remarkable capacity for adaption, discernment, boldness, spontaneity, laughter, creativity, adventure, curiosity, seizing the moment, boundless energy, and untainted optimism, so it would appear that there is a lot we can learn from children. But there is not so much they can learn from us.

I have never been particularly enamored of babies or very young children, and marvel at those who have the energy and commitment to accommodate and accept responsibility for the influencing of young minds and unformed personalities. Apart from the attraction I hold towards teaching *dysfunctional* adults like myself, I have always been strongly opposed to training young children to sing too early. Subsequently, I do not take on students below the age of fourteen—at least that was so until four extraordinary 11-year-olds, two 12-year-olds, and a 13-year-old all found their way to my door within the space of one month. Suddenly I was faced with the 21st century phenomenon of the *child star*, forcing me to rethink my approach to it all.

Teaching versus training
The only child star I remember when I was growing up was Shirley Temple, whose curls, cuteness, and innocent precociousness had the world falling at her tapping feet and cooing over her infantile antics. What made her so appealing was the fact that she was unspoiled and this, I believe, was because she only emulated characters of her own age. Today agencies and corporations scout and mentor toddlers and teens with big, brassy voices and commercial viability, seducing parents into believing that if their child is destined for success, he or she must be exhibiting brilliance and theatrical *sass* before puberty. This is a dangerous message that is wrongly encouraging parents to seek vocal training for their children rather than *musicianship* and *vocal expression*.

If a child is unusually mature vocally, it is easy to ignore or override the growing up or developmental stages that are natural and necessary for all children. *Teaching* provides knowledge, whereas *training* disciplines the already knowledgeable people in the techniques of executing a skill. Teaching is broader and more general, which places the emphasis on ideas, knowledge, and wisdom, stimulating the need to *know*, whereas training shapes the habits of an individual and is usually aimed at a specific and often commercial area of skill. This places the emphasis on *ability* and the need to *do*. I now realise that I am not remotely opposed to the teaching of children, but rather to the vocal training of young voices for the purpose of specialisation and/or commercialisation. Although there are always exceptions to the rule, training a child to sing operatically is like training a child to body-build, in the way that it pushes muscles to develop sooner than they are ready, resulting in premature maturation and therefore limited longevity. This is not in any way to say that children should not be singing or physically exercising - quite the opposite in fact. But the current obsession the world holds for *bankable commodity* is undermining and ignoring the vital developmental stages necessary to nurture young voices.

One trick pony
One noticeably absent element in the current education of young singers is an emphasis on the importance of becoming a proficient musician, e.g., through playing an instrument, sight-reading, aural precision, and composing one's own original music. Although children have an amazing

capacity to create, listen, imitate, and memorise, without any logical explanations to guide them, the currently convenient and lazy method of learning songs via a backing track with an often suspect guide vocal to imitate is breeding a generation of extremely unmusical and gimmicky performers with no real theoretical foundation or technical understanding. If basic musicianship is not fostered and encouraged in the early stages of musical development, it is so much harder to access and utilise later in life.

The term *one trick pony* is generally used as a disparaging description of someone of limited ability who works very effectively within a specific parameter but lacks the versatility, flexibility and imagination to move from this place. In music, a *one trick pony* is an artist who uses the same musical riffs and licks in everything he or she sings, which although initially dazzling, eventually becomes tedious and predictable. The current musical climate is encouraging this very thing by rewarding young singers for emulating their older counterparts and directly or indirectly placing the emphasis on high, loud, sophisticated, and marketable, rather than sensitive, musical, age appropriate, and individual.

> ## "A teacher affects eternity; he can never tell where his influence stops."
> *- Henry Adams*

As long as a teacher has realistic expectations of a young voice, there is no danger of causing damage. But it must be understood that children process information differently to adults and, therefore, the way in which they are taught must cater to and accommodate this fact. Today, children are pushed harder than ever before to *perform* or *measure up* in what is fast becoming an *adult* world, making the need to keep things positive, light, and fun all the more important. So what should we do to allow a gifted child the maximum opportunity to develop musically? How can we enhance without complicating, assist without interfering, support without taking control, and guide without forcing our own agenda? In my opinion, the best a teacher or a parent can offer is a patient and unobtrusive presence that gives the child a safe environment and the freedom to creatively *explore* on his or her own terms, in his or her own time.

When Tim first sang for me I could not quite get my head around the sound I was hearing. Although he was only twenty years old, he had the vocal quality of a little old man who was past his prime. His vocal tone was forced and coreless and there was a disconcerting wobble, suggesting the kind of disconnect that often occurs with the overuse of the voice, or an aging support system. On discussion, Tim told me that he had been a soloist in a children's choir and had been training classically with a middle-aged opera singer since he was about thirteen. This immediately gave me insight into how and why he sounded this way. Children are extremely impressionable and imitate what they see and hear, and for years he had been emulating the mature and operatically produced sound of his teacher without the muscle development to support it. Subsequently his vocal habits were firmly entrenched, which left his young voice lacking its own particular style and authenticity. Miguel, on the other hand, is quite a different story.

Not so long ago, Miguel's father called me to ask if I would take on his 11-year-old son as my student. According to his father, Miguel was extremely talented, had his own fan base on YouTube, and was also being 'head hunted' by two of the best record companies in Asia. However, his parents both felt that there was no hurry for this and wanted to spend time nurturing his talent before placing him under the inevitable pressure of stardom. Miguel was everything his father had described and more, with an almost pitch perfect voice, an extensive range, complete control of his vocal registers, stylistic versatility, and the ability to concentrate and focus longer than most adults. For this reason, I teach him as though he is an adult, as everything about him suggests maturity and discernment. But, interestingly, there is no sign of precociousness or forced development, despite the fact that this beautiful little Filipino boy already knows exactly who he is and what he wants for his future.

When Jeanne came to work with me she had small vocal nodules and a leading role in a musical to prepare for. An exquisitely beautiful young girl of French/Lebanese descent, Jeanne learned the hard way that screaming at soccer matches and incorrect vocal production would never serve the performing career she desired. Three months of technical work and a change in awareness and attitude saw the last of the nodules and the beginnings of a fresh and lovely young voice.

Mackenzie takes her lessons very seriously and only with great teasing from me will her divine brown eyes and solemn demeanor threaten to lighten up. Although generally shy and introspective, she has occasionally left me astounded with her astute technical questioning and impromptu rock impersonations of Adele.

Rohan fidgets incessantly and cannot stand still for more than a few minutes, but when he opens his mouth to sing, the heavens open up and angels literally come out to play. Scales do not interest him, but if the technical work is cleverly disguised to look and sound like a song, he is immediately transfixed and transformed.

Ashlynn is 13 and engages with people openly and honestly making her intensely likeable and a joy to teach. Highly musical with a beautiful but young voice, she appears to be devoid of the usual barriers many children of her age carry, which makes her into a kind of musical sponge. Everything I ask her to do, she does, every concept I present, she understands, and every creative risk I ask her to take is met with a sense of humour and adventure.

Every one of these children is talented and every one of these children is different and every one of these children has the personality and vocal ability to become successful in the future. Children do not need to *master* a skill but they do need to *see, hear,* and *feel* new concepts before they can fully understand them. Teach them to *feel* their bodies, teach them to *feel* their breath and teach them to *feel* all the things they carry within themselves, and then allow them to explore and experiment with who and what they discover. From this place, children will develop their own motivations and form their own conclusions, which will determine the direction they will ultimately choose to take.

We all enter the world unadulterated and intact with a propensity for joy and optimism, but perversely allow this to become layered, camouflaged and ultimately traded in for the grand title of *responsible grown up.* We then proceed to spend a lifetime wading through the prison of logic, rationale, objectivity, and intellect in a never-ending pilgrimage to rediscover the place from whence we came. This challenging journey is inevitable and each and every child will embark on it somehow, somewhere, sometime.

Childhood is so precious and unbelievably short, so for now, let them *play*.

NOTES:

11

EVERYBODY SAYS, "DON'T!"
Much Ado about Nothing?

"Progress always involves risk."
- Frederick Wilcox

A world of difference - The things that make the world so interesting are the differing racial, cultural, religious, political, generational, and ethical opinions that circulate within it, but human perception is subjective and differs wildly among individuals. Many points of view contain at least some element of wisdom, but over-generalisations and the irresolvable projection into the *unknown* have a tendency to imbue fear and limitation with more than the potential to crush an adventurous spirit. It is important to recognize that there is a huge difference between common sense based on tangible reality, and the irrationalities of superstition and rumor. Many times I have heard myself repeating things I have been told simply because I respect the person they came from. Sometimes they are founded in truth, but often they are not. Parents teach their children what their parents taught them, and these children pass it on to the next generation, and so the cycle continues for as long as we choose not to question the truth of what it is we are passing on. The difficulty lies in the fact that this behavior has been an accepted part of our reality for so long that we hardly recognise it is there or that we, ourselves, play an unknowing part in keeping it alive.

When I was in fifth grade my teacher stood us all in a straight line, whispered something into the ear of the first student and asked him to pass it on to the person next to him where it was then passed on to the end of the line. The last student was then asked to repeat what had been said to see if and how the sentence had changed on its journey. When the teacher finally told us what the words were in the beginning, I was astounded at how distorted it had become after being repeated by only 15 students. This lesson was memorable and most revealing as to how quickly and easily information becomes distorted or misunderstood when passed from person to person. Depending on the nature of the information, this is then colored by the fact that the world is fundamentally conditioned to see the cloud rather than the silver lining and seems to thrive on what might be seen as a *soap opera* mentality.

"If drama were vodka, we would all be wasted "
- Anonymous

From the moment a singer discovers he or she has a voice worth training, drama and tension begin. The body IS the instrument, and so illness can and will directly or indirectly affect the voice, making small irritations like coughs, colds, and allergies seem like a matter of life and death. This shines a glaring light on the need for all performers to become clear on what is within their control and what is not, as physical and emotional well-being relies on the psychological state of the individual. Environment and health are the things that can be controlled to one degree or another, but what cannot be controlled is the unknown. *What ifs* and *maybes* act as a creative *cancer,* eating away at the very energy needed to keep a singer centered and in the *zone,* yet these questions only need be addressed if and when the situation arises. Comments such as *"Chest voice will give you nodules, vibrato isn't good, never sing to the extremes of your range, classical singing is the only safe style, practicing for an hour is too much, pop music is for people who can't sing, stick to one style, belting will ruin your voice"* are just some of the sweeping generalizations uttered in the name of correct singing. But under scrutiny it becomes clear that these statements are founded either in ignorance, extreme cases of vocal abuse, or the results of compromised technique in the individual.

As mentioned in earlier chapters, we are born with a voice in order to communicate and our ability to communicate is integral to survival; therefore, it is not the natural state of the vocal apparatus to be constricted or compromised. In my opinion, many vocal perceptions are unknowingly based on the *give a dog a bad name syndrome*, where negative case studies unfairly undermine the validity and safety of specific registers and genres of music. It is not uncommon in Australia to see people jogging on the hard pavement wearing one or two knee supports. Although I cannot know the circumstances, I have to assume that they have some form of weakness or injury, which is probably caused by running in the first place. Does this mean that running is inherently bad, or is the athlete ignoring the symptoms of his injury and should either rest the injury or find a more supportive way to exercise? Vocal damage is mostly due to ignoring symptoms of strain and fatigue that can be a result of any number of things. Incorrect vocal placement will negatively affect the coordination of all the technical elements required for safe singing, and it is ridiculous to blame one particular style, register or genre for it. It is the *intelligence* behind what we do that matters and intelligence is based on knowledge, experience, and reliable research. "Don't walk around with bare feet, don't go to bed with wet hair, don't eat spicy food, don't drink alcohol, stay away from dairy foods, get at least eight hours sleep, stay away from open windows, don't drink caffeine, always wear a scarf, don't cough, never clear your throat, don't eat chocolate or bananas, whispering is bad, don't eat before you sing" are some suggestions offered by doctors and teachers, and although many are supported by reliable factual evidence, others are arguable and dependent on the constitution and sensitivities of the individual.

"Stress is an ignorant state. It believes that everything is an emergency"
- Natalie Goldberg

Stress is often a direct result of fear of the future or the unknown. "Could be," "should be," "might be," and "what if" all preempt questions about a future that has not yet happened, rendering them impossible to resolve. The only thing you can do is to prepare for life and its circumstances to the best of your ability, and the rest is beyond your control. There are many things a singer can do to deal with the rigors and challenges of keeping the voice healthy, and one of them is to listen to your body and learn to support its needs as they arise.

- *Train your voice regularly with a qualified teacher you trust and respect.*

- *Warm up properly before you sing.*

- *Keep excessive talking to a minimum, particularly over loud music or overly ambient environments.*

- *Avoid places where there is smoke or haze.*

- *Regulate the amount of extreme singing or belting you do.*

- *Mark or sing softly when you first learn a piece of music before introducing power or volume*

- *Beware of a constant cough or excessive throat clearing, as it is very abrasive for the vocal cords.*

- *Rest vocally if you have signs of fatigue and if the problem persists, see a qualified ENT or laryngologist for advice.*

- *Avoid emotional confrontations and work daily towards maintaining a relaxed state of mind.*

- *Spend time on your own and get plenty of sleep.*

- *Exercise regularly.*

Irreconcilable differences

Unfortunately, many modern-day environments have a negative impact on the body's hydration levels and are quite simply, irreconcilable differences. Having subjected myself to the tropical climate of Singapore for the past seven years, I would have to say that the greatest challenge for me has been trying to avoid the freezing temperatures and dehydrating effects of centralized air conditioning. Although a welcome relief to relentless humidity, air conditioning is renowned for aggravating certain health issues and contaminating the air with microorganisms and mould. This is not good news for people who suffer from asthma, bronchitis, or other respiratory illnesses, and can often be responsible for serious lung infections and other allergic reactions. Neither is it kind to the human voice, but as we are all born with an immune system designed to combat illness and disease, it is wise to focus on building its strength and to put the emphasis on prevention rather than cure.

Water is paramount for the healthy functioning of the human body and for a singer it is extremely important that the mucous membrane on the vocal folds remain sufficiently hydrated for correct phonation. It is not generally recognized that the water we drink does not go directly to or touch the vocal mechanism. Instead it travels to all other parts of the body first and only if there is sufficient hydration left over will it then accommodate the needs of the cords. The inhaling of steam from a bowl of water or spending twenty minutes in a steam room at the gym, however, will provide hydration and relief by allowing the vapor to go directly to the area.

If you work where there is air conditioning

1. *Use a humidifier to add moisture to the space you are in.*

2. *Keep the temperature as high as you can to avoid the extreme changes when you go outside again.*

3. *If you have a ceiling fan, use this instead.*

4. *Whenever you have a break, try to go outside to get some fresh air.*

5. Keep your neck and body warm by using a scarf.

6. Drink plenty of fluids (preferably room temperature).

7. Join a gym and regularly use the steam room.

8. Try to avoid the need to sleep with air conditioning by cooling down the room an hour before you go to bed.

Countless times I have had singers come to a lesson vocally strained or voiceless after a show rehearsal or a band gig, and nine times out of ten it will be due to an inadequate or non-existent fold back system. The human voice is an acoustic instrument and therefore cannot be expected to compete with electric guitars, keyboards or drum kits. Although singers are amplified through a microphone, this does not necessarily mean that they can hear themselves over the other instruments, and so the tendency will be to push or force the voice to be heard. Those who believe they can maintain a healthy voice under such conditions are sadly mistaken, and must make the inclusion of suitable fold back monitors a non-negotiable element when working. Show rehearsals are often conducted in venues ill equipped to support the acoustic voice and can either be vacuous and booming or carpeted and *dry*. Whether the room is swallowing up the voice, or the space is sucking the life out of the sound, the singer will tend to try to make amends for this and end up using his or her voice incorrectly. As your vocal apparatus is housed within your body, it is not possible to hear your voice in the same way the audience does, and therefore it is an integral part of technique to learn to work with the *sensation* of the sound rather than what you are hearing. No two rehearsal rooms will have the same acoustic makeup, so it can be more than daunting when the sounds you are hearing yourself make are not what you are used to experiencing in your lessons or in your chosen place of practice. If you feel as though you are over-working your voice, you are, and if you feel that the sound is free and balanced, it is.

"Nature itself is the best physician"
- Hippocrates

If the human body is indeed an instrument, and we *are* essentially *what* we eat, then the quality of the food we consume will have a huge bearing on how our immune systems handle physical, emotional and environmental stresses. Many processed foods are acidic and known to create excessive phlegm and irritation of the mucous membranes in the throat and the mouth. The types of foods renowned for this can differ from person to person, but there is wide opinion that some should be avoided when performing or, in more extreme cases, completely removed from one's diet. Dairy products such as milk, cheese, yoghurt, ice cream and high fat foods like chocolate, butter and cream, are best taken in moderation as they coat the throat and mouth. And there is caution against regularly eating very spicy foods as they can create acid reflux and have the potential to irritate or damage the pharynx and the vocal cords. Caffeinated drinks like tea, coffee, soft drinks, and alcohol all have a dehydrating effect, so singers should be mindful of whether and how they impact their voices, and regulate accordingly.

Once food has been cooked it can lose up to 85 percent of its nutritional value, as heat changes the molecular structure, killing its life force and destroying beneficial enzymes. Thus the title of *dead food* among raw food advocates, as the digestive system has to work harder and longer to get nutrition and energy from it, making our bodies feel heavy and stagnant. It is the raw and unprocessed foods that are considered to be *alive,* and subsequently the most beneficial for overall health and wellbeing. By including more salads, vegetables, fruits, nuts, whole grains, and proteins into your diet, the immune system is more capable of fighting illness and disease. Fresh fruit and vegetable juices are not only another source of fluid intake, but also a great way to fulfill the daily nutritional requirements without having to consume huge amounts of food.

A handy hint - *If suffering from excessive mucus or coating in the mouth, mix some lime or lemon juice with warm water and aim past the teeth to the back of the throat with a syringe to dissolve fat or phlegm.*

Some remedies that are worse than the disease
Many cold and flu medications contain agents and caffeine that dehydrate the mucus membranes, so there is the need for caution and research into the products you are taking when you are ill. Because of the blood-thinning agents, anti-inflammatory drugs like aspirin or in extreme cases of steroids, like cortisone, can make a singer susceptible to vocal fold hemorrhage and should be avoided. It is important to recognise that there is *muscle fatigue* and *tissue fatigue* and therefore the treatment for them will differ. Muscular fatigue happens when the muscles of the vocal system are over-used, so the singer should work on stretching and relaxing the jaw, neck, and shoulders. Tissue fatigue, on the other hand, is caused by excessive destruction or inflammation of the cells that make up the vocal fold tissue, so remedies like steam inhalation and saltwater gargle can be helpful to hydrate the voice and clean out the nasal passages. Many throat lozenges are nothing but great-tasting *placebos,* with little clinical proof that ingredients such as menthol, eucalyptus, vitamin C, echinacea, and zinc, help in reducing the symptoms of a sore throat. On the other hand, the *super food*, Manuka honey, is revered for its antiviral and antibacterial activity and can be taken by the teaspoon to soothe and counteract just about any ailment. Antibiotics, sleeping tablets and antidepressants do not treat the cause of illnesses and while they are suppressing the symptoms, they are also attacking the immune system.

Keep it simple
I grew up running around in bare feet, always went to bed with wet hair, and still love sleeping with the windows open no matter how cold the weather. It is freezing air conditioning, fluorescent lighting, processed food, caffeine, late nights, and stress that will agitate my system, so I avoid them wherever I can. Others seem to thrive on city living and external stimulus, so I can only deduce that as long as you are happy and healthy, there is no need to change the way you live your life. Read the signs, find the solutions that work for you, do what you need to do - but above all, keep it simple.

12
YOU AND ME AGAINST THE WORLD
The Universe is Friendly

"Nothing in life is to be feared. It is only to be understood."
- Marie Curie

I used to dream of falling. Every night it was the same: Falling for what seemed like an eternity, hitting the ground with enormous force and being jolted awake with my lungs gasping for air and my heart pounding. Eventually the nightmares ended, but if I look back at my life thus far, I can see that I have spent much of my time fighting the terrifying feeling of falling. I don't remember exactly when I became unsure of myself but I do remember standing in front of a crowd of people fearlessly showcasing my vocal talents and loving every minute I was there. I also remember my horror, at the age of 11, when I opened my mouth to sing only to find that my sweet and sunny voice had been replaced by some kind of apprehensive imposter. Overnight I appeared to have become a weak and timid shadow of myself, and have been searching for the child I remember ever since. Thankfully, courage is the one thing that was never in short supply for me, which I'm sure is why I stand where I am today.

Unless you have been lucky enough to grow up in an empowering environment, or are one of the few who thrive on being the centre of attention, you will have experienced some form of performance anxiety or stage fright. Whether mild or chronic, fear of failure and rejection tends to govern our lives, and many of us carry a false sense of worthlessness because of it. In our formative years, *positive reinforcement* is essential for the development of healthy boundaries and self esteem, but *feedback* that is served up negatively can create a void that can often take a lifetime to fill or resolve. That being said, in spite of conditioning, in spite of trauma, and in spite of where we are on our journey, I know with absolute certainty that the paralysing tentacles of fear can be transcended if their true illusory nature can be understood.

That's history!
Going back into the past is only useful if you are seeking to locate the *cause* of fear and want to release whatever it is that is preventing you from having the kind of life you want for yourself. Otherwise, it simply serves to perpetuate resentment and what is commonly known as a *victim consciousness*. So often, the things others say to us are filtered incorrectly by our own warped perceptions and low opinions of ourselves. I remember a day when I was 12 years old and my mother casually told me that she couldn't wait for me to grow up, as I had been such an odd looking baby. She punctuated this comment by announcing that my sisters were pretty but I was *striking* and *unusual*. Her words cut me deeply as I understood this to mean that I was unattractive and, subsequently, undesirable. Throughout my teens, twenties, and thirties I was obsessed with obtaining all things *pretty*. Blonde hair, slim body, tanned skin, and fashionable clothes sent me into a spiral of compulsive spending, to no real avail. One day, many years later, I happened to come across a baby photo of myself and was immediately drawn to the child with the huge eyes, rosebud mouth and seriously chubby cheeks. All these years I had believed I was plain and unattractive, and all these years I had neglected to remember that not only had my mother told me on numerous occasions how beautiful I was, but also that she deemed striking and unusual to be far more interesting than pretty. In my late teens, I allowed yet another situation to sink nails into the coffin of my self-esteem when my first serious boyfriend told me, one day, that the song I was singing to him sounded horrible and that I should stop. I was mortified and never sang impromptu again. Yet again I had allowed myself to overlook the numerous compliments I had received from other reliable sources about my voice, choosing only to dwell on the destructive comment of an insensitive male.

Each of us has a responsibility when criticising or reprimanding another, as unless information is given constructively the person on the receiving end can easily interpret it as rejection, and it is a deep and often irrational fear of rejection that breeds and fosters all emotional dysfunction. At the most primal level, acceptance and validation from our families, friends, colleagues, and society guarantees us happiness and, in essence, survival. Rejection, on the other hand, is most often perceived to bring pain, loneliness, humiliation, and possible death.

Fight or flight
The term *fight or flight* describes a mechanism in the body that enables humans and animals to quickly mobilise large amounts of energy in order to cope with any kind of threat or danger to his or her survival and, whenever this happens, an automatic sequence of events is set in motion.

- The nervous system is put on alert
- Adrenaline is released
- The heart beats harder and faster
- The breath becomes more rapid.

Fight manifests in aggressive, combative behaviour and *flight* results in the withdrawal or retreat from a potentially threatening situation. A third response that usually comes before fight or flight is *freezing,* which is what a deer or rabbit does when paralysed by the headlights of an oncoming car. This allows time to assess the situation before attempting the further actions of fighting or retreating. However, even though this response is automatic, the part of the brain that initiates it cannot distinguish between a *real* threat and a *perceived* threat and, therefore, is unreliable and inaccurate. More often than not, the situation we are defending ourselves from poses no threat to survival at all and is only a *false alarm,* which then becomes the catalyst for behaviours contrary to the ones we wish to create. Learning to understand *why this is so* becomes an informative and fascinating study in itself.

Freeze
Etienne was a young and brilliant Singaporean doctor, blessed with a photographic memory, stunning good looks, and holding an obsession for all things musical theatre. Every time he opened his mouth to sing, however, a strange metamorphosis would take place. His eyes became glazed and fixed, his neck would strain upwards, his body became rigid, his face drained of all emotion, and his voice became a virtual monotone. In essence, he would enter a trance-like state where he appeared to be dazed and immobilised. Although he was desperate to sing professionally, the action of it seemed to trigger some kind of repressed trauma that would shut him down every time he tried. When I asked him to tell me about his early singing experiences he described numerous, colourful Karaoke parties that were held at his home when he was around five years old, and how his parents would drag him and his sister out of bed in the wee hours of the morning, attach them to a microphone, and force them to entertain a delighted and inebriated crowd until the *kiddie novelty* wore off. This continued for several years, leaving Etienne with the defensive behaviour of *freezing* every time he stood in front of an audience.

Fight

I have always loved the rehearsal process, and consider the discovery of unknown chunks of myself in a rehearsal room in the bowels of a theatre to be a sheer luxury. On the other hand, performing for an audience can throw me into an abyss of insecurity and terror. Many times I have experienced panic attacks and insomnia for weeks before a performance, leaving me confused, frustrated, and exhausted. Medically there is nothing wrong with me, as the attacks are related to events and end immediately once they are over. As I learn more about myself, and dig deeper into the irrationalities of my subconscious, I have come to understand that performing acts as a *trigger* for several deep insecurities I developed when I was a child. Perversely, I perceived the practicing of my craft and rehearsing with others to be creative, supportive, and fun but, on the other hand, when I had to present the finished product to others, I felt an unbearable pressure to prove that I deserved to be there. "You are a *Colliver* and you will uphold the family name" was the *mantra* my parents would regularly use when I was growing up. These words in themselves should have been inspirational, imbuing pride, motivation, and family loyalty, but as they were only used as a severe reprimand when I had failed to do them proud, I incorrectly learned that I would always let those who put their faith in me *down*. Consequently, every time I placed myself in a position of *proving my worth,* a downward spiral of crippling fear would consume me again. It was never an option for me to lie down and die or run away from the source of my distress, which is not to say that standing my ground and battling on regardless was the right approach to take, but simply the way my subconscious tends to deal with confrontational situations.

Flight

Glenda stood at the piano, singing the scale I had just given her with a beautiful, rich, and luxurious soprano voice but, as we approached the higher notes, she suddenly became anxious, her voice subdued, and her left leg began to shake uncontrollably. I stopped to ask what was distressing her, and she answered that she always became agitated and scared in this part of her voice but really did not understand why. After a lengthy discussion Glenda revealed that, as she was a *lazy* singer who enjoyed the lower resonances in her voice more than the high, her first teacher would tap her on the left leg with a ruler to help her create the necessary energy to access the upper notes. The teacher would become more and more excited the higher she sang and, without realising, would hit her leg harder and harder. Glenda consequently learned to associate pain with the upper part of her voice and her body would predictably assume the posture of *retreat* every time she approached the higher frequencies.

The Reptilian Brain

In the deep of the human brain is an ancient layer called the *Reptilian Brain,* which controls the primal and instinctive behaviour of a human being. It is not capable of *feeling* or *thinking,* as its only function is to spring into defensive action whenever and wherever there is a threat. This renders it cold, rigid, territorial, aggressive, paranoid, and obsessive and, as many of the pressures of today trigger this response, most of us are going through our lives in a permanent state of *defense.*

The Neo-cortex

The neo-cortex part of the brain is involved in the higher functions of sensory perception, language, motor skills, and the ability to process thoughts and emotions logically and rationally. Love, empathy, compassion, and spiritual aspiration are all nurtured here but, unfortunately, most of us are governed by our primitive responses and cannot reap the benefits of its deep potential for wisdom and joy.

A vicious cycle

Fear is a vital response to physical danger, but unfortunately this response can be triggered within us where there is, in fact, no threat whatsoever to our safety or survival. This kind of fear occurs in the mind and is a projected thought about what *might* happen in the future, creating an irresolvable cycle of *what ifs* and *maybes*. These negative *probabilities* have not yet happened and, in all likelihood, won't. That being the case, this type of illusory fear is only:

- **F**alse
- **E**vidence
- **A**ppearing
- **R**eal

Fear is like a merry-go-round in the way that it turns around and around on itself, with no ability to do anything other than to move in a perpetually closed and never-ending circle. It subsequently prevents us from taking *action,* and where there is no *action* it is not possible to gain *experience.* Where there is no *experience*, there can be no *skill,* and where there is no *skill*, there is no *confidence.* Where there is no *confidence*, *fear* is prevalent, and so the cycle continues until such time as we are able to change the way in which we respond to situations and experiences, as illustrated in the diagram below.

© Vikas Malkani 2008 www.soulcentre.org

It is essential to understand that fear only appears when something *big* is about to happen, and this uneasy feeling is a message to let you know that you are now out of your comfort zone and ready for some kind of meaningful *change* in your life. Rather than to trying to overcome fear, we must train ourselves to take action despite its immobilising effects. When action is taken, experience is gained, and when experience is gained, ability and confidence will all rise. When confidence rises, there is the courage to take action, and this courage leads to more action, which then leads to more experience, and so the cycle continues.

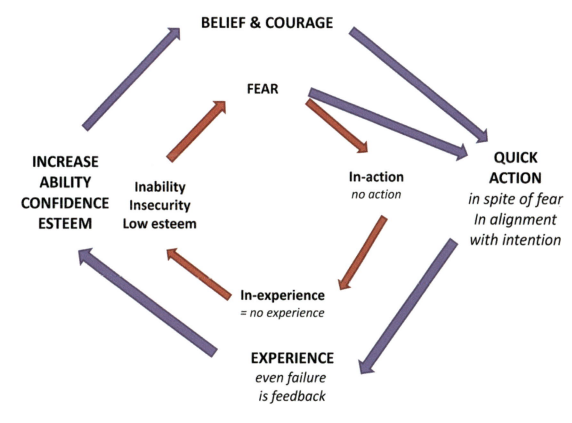

© Vikas Malkani 2008 www.soulcentre.org

Learning through adversity
None of us likes to make mistakes but, like them or not, they are an essential and extremely relevant part of the *learning process*. For many singers, *rehearsing* a piece of music is psychologically very different to *performing* a piece of music, and they are often taken by surprise by the challenges that arise in front of an audience. Performing experience cannot be gained anywhere *but* in front of an audience and, therefore, public mistakes are to be expected and must be embraced. If this is not understood and accepted, the whole encounter will be pointless and traumatic.

Perfectionism
I have heard many a student justify dwelling on a sabotaged performance with the proud statement, "It's because I'm a perfectionist!" as if this were a desirable and necessary ingredient for success.

Striving for *perfection* is not the same as striving for *excellence,* and understanding the difference is crucial to physical, emotional, and artistic progress. *Perfection* is a *belief system* about yourself and others that creates compulsive self-criticism and a rejection of anything that does not meet the highest of standards. No matter how hard they work, perfectionists are not able to feel pride or satisfaction with their efforts, as the judgemental aspect of their nature is always reminding them that they could have done better. Nothing will ever be good enough for these students and, therefore, they create a self-imposed prison of anxiety, failure, separation, and disappointment. Thankfully, this kind of self-absorbed attack on oneself can be transcended in a moment if striving for *perfection* can be traded in for working towards *excellence.*

Excellence
Those who strive for excellence understand the need for a *creative process,* and take enormous pleasure in the hard work and effort necessary to attain their *goal*s. When the motivation becomes the desire to *master* a skill, it is easy to accept any mistakes along the way as part of the journey, enabling the student to learn from them with minimal feelings of failure and unworthiness. Taking personal responsibility for mistakes or shortcomings firstly allows us to seek out the reason they occurred, and then to make moves to avoid repeating them. Mistakes happen for many reasons and take differing amounts of time to resolve, so intelligence and discernment about a suitable remedy are needed if they are to be rectified.

Overcoming the fear of rejection:

1. *Take note of when and where you feel you are operating from fear.*

2. *Notice the situations or environments that make you feel uneasy or unsafe.*

3. *Ask yourself what these feelings are founded upon, and if indeed, they are rational.*

4. *Identify the people from whom you fear rejection and ask yourself if and why you feel these people are rejecting you.*

5. *Find constructive behaviours to implement into your daily life by replacing negative thoughts with those of safety and trust, and by looking for the positives in all situations.*

6. *Analyse any situations that have had a negative impact on you and see what you have learned from those experiences.*

7. *Look at all challenging situations as an opportunity to grow.*

Through giving we receive
How different would our lives be if we could not only tolerate rejection but actually learn to embrace it by allowing others to disagree with us, or by accepting that the answer is *no*, and still believe in our own worthiness? Nothing short of a shift in perception will suffice, and this shift begins with the

knowledge that stage fright is simply an *imagined barrier* between the audience and ourselves, fueled by one question only - *will they like me?* This question places us in the position of *taking* rather than one of seeking to *connect* and *communicate*; but in all fairness, we are all conditioned and encouraged to develop what is known as an *identity* or *ego,* which is no more than multiple rationalisations and justifications for *what* and *who we think we are,* or *should be.* Diligent, intelligent, talented, reliable, honest, sensitive, prosperous, attractive, innovative, and so on, are all labels we bestow upon ourselves and others, which unfortunately demand constant reinforcement and validation from something or someone outside of ourselves. This in itself breeds *isolation* and *self-absorption.*

No matter whether you are a beginner or a seasoned professional, performance anxiety affects almost everyone, and the level of paranoid ingenuity we create to defeat ourselves is nothing short of astounding. Although you are standing on the stage, the experience is not about you *alone*, but rather about you in *relationship with another.* Surely if you did not feel that you had something to offer, you would not be standing there in the first place, so *what* is it you wish to share and *how* do you wish to present it to your audience?

Those in the audience who have come to enjoy your performance are not only there to listen, but also to be touched and inspired. Small mistakes either go unnoticed or are irrelevant to those listening for something far more valuable and important, so allow them to pass and try to be present in every new moment. Your voice is only a *vehicle* for the music they hear, and if you can allow yourself to be a *conduit,* you will find yourself *being sung.* When this happens, fear and separation begin to disappear, and when they do, Etienne will stop believing he is being dragged out of bed to *entertain the troops*, Glenda will know that she is no longer being *abused* when she hits her high notes, and I will cease to believe that I will ever let those who believe in me *down*. There is nothing for us to do other than remove the blocks that prevent us from appreciating and sharing all the gifts we have to offer.

Exercises:

a) *Remind yourself that you have prepared and practiced to the best of your ability and, although you may still have much to learn, you have done your best for where you are now in your development.*

b) *Do not treat a performance like a technical lesson. The time for practicing is over and although you will still need to be aware of your technique, you can now allow your muscle memory to take over and concentrate on communicating with your audience.*

c) *Constructively remind yourself of one or two things you would like to achieve and avoid before going onstage, and then try to implement them throughout your performance.*

d) *Do not try to second-guess the audience. You cannot know what they are thinking and, if you try, you will not be focused or authentic in your communication. Concentrate only on the act of giving.*

e) Do not allow your personal critic to give a running commentary on how you believe you are doing, as this kind of thinking takes you out of the present moment and into the sabotaging thoughts of a possible future. This will most certainly interrupt the natural flow of your creativity, and your fears will inevitably become a self-fulfilling prophecy.

f) Do not magnify your mistakes. Take note of them, learn from them, and let them go.

g) Be gracious and accept the praise you receive from your audience. Allow them to share their experience with you without any self-deprecation or deflection.

h) Continually remind yourself that you are doing what you love to do and what you want to do.

You have worked hard, so celebrate and let yourself be celebrated.

NOTES:

13

ME, MYSELF AND I
Who's Running this Show?

"You have to leave the city of your comfort and go into the wilderness of your intuition if you wish to discover yourself"
- Alan Alda

The human mind creates on several levels, some that we are aware of and others that we are not, but unless this is understood it is easy to become confused and downhearted when actions and events in our lives seemingly refuse to shift or change. The totality of our consciousness consists of three levels of awareness: the *subconscious,* the *conscious,* and the *super conscious.* And although these are all part of one mind, we are conditioned to utilise one more than the others, which creates imbalance and disharmony among them.

Conscious (me)
The level of consciousness from which we receive guidance is the *conscious* state that usually guides our daily decisions. This guidance is received via the input of the five senses, which analyse the *perceived* facts and make decisions based on this information. However, the conscious state is incapable of perceiving the big picture or the *interconnectedness* of all things and is severely limited by an analytical nature that only sees things as *separate* and *distinct*. This renders it co-dependent and strongly influenced by the opinions of others, clouding its ability to recognise the truth of any given situation. As the conscio*us* mind is the only part of reality we can see, we rely more heavily on it than any other level of awareness - but it is only the tip of the iceberg, and riddled with misinformation.

Subconscious (myself)
The subconscious mind only has a dim level of awareness and is the repository of all remembered experience*s*, the impressions of those experiences, and the tendencies awakened or reinforced by those impressions. Every experience we have ever had, every thought, and every positive and negative perception lives in the subconscious mind, thus determining our patterns of thought and behaviour. The subconscious, however, is relatively unrestricted by the rigidity of logic and allows a certain freedom of ideas. This freedom borders on intuition, but can easily be mistaken for *intuitive guidance*, when, in fact, it is only the influence of *subconscious preconditioning*. There are many parts of our subconscious that are too painful or frightening to face, and so remain unaddressed until we develop phobias or illness. It is, however, an enormous source of untapped potential and, when accessed, can unlock avenues of unlimited power.

Super conscious (I)
Intuition and heightened mental clarity come from super conscious awareness whose nature is to see all things holistically, where a problem and its solution are perceived as one and the same. *Intuition* is the receiver of ideas and images without knowing exactly how and where they come from. We simply sense that an idea or an inexplicable feeling of *knowing* is not being sent from the conscious mind, and is often referred to as a *gut feeling, sixth sense, instinct*, or the *inner voice*.

We all have internal voices that feed us messages about ourselves and these voices will either be empowering or disempowering, depending on whether the conversation is positive or negative. The voice that runs an incessant commentary on your failings and shortcomings is the negative feedback of the *lower self* or ego, but the voice that speaks rationally and positively is that of the *higher self* or *intuition*. Although the conscious and subconscious minds are, in fact, connected, they often work in opposition to each other, creating emotional havoc and an uneasy sense of disconnect. How often has one part of you wanted to do something one way, only to be contradicted by another part of you that believes you should behave differently? By moving our awareness inward, we can begin to make the *unconscious* parts of us *conscious*, so that eventually all can begin to work together.

The conscious mind has been programmed to focus on what we *lack,* and on any given day we will all entertain hundreds of disempowering thoughts ranging from mild berating to chronic judgement and reprimand. These thoughts will rampage through our minds with astounding strength and alarming regularity until we understand that there is only one thing that will slow them down and eventually stop them in their tracks. S*top voicing them*! When words are given a platform on which to play, they become stronger, and when they are not given this platform, they begin to weaken and eventually change their tone altogether. Only when this happens can the quiet, wise, and noble voice of intuition be heard. Differentiating the states of mind and training one to become stronger than the other is the first step towards converting disempowering behaviour into progressive and inspirational authenticity. The conscious mind has an obsessive investment in *separation* and deeming things *right* and *wrong,* and is not an advocate for creativity and vision, but the voice that inspires *courage, passion, confidence,* and *joy* most definitely is. From here, all things are possible.

Observation

The best way to access your subconscious is to become sensitive and receptive to everything around you by observing what you feel and what your internal voices say to you about these experiences. All change begins with observation. You cannot change what you have not yet recognised, and you cannot recognise something that you are not consciously seeking; therefore, *waking up* is reliant on several crucial things.

1. *The ability to listen to and be interested in what others have to say*

2. *Curiosity about how and why things are the way they are*

3. *An open mind to new possibilities and experiences*

4. *Empathy for different behaviours and attitudes*

5. *Allowing the positive input of other people*

6. *Being comfortable with not knowing or being out of control*

7. *An awareness of how your behaviour and attitudes affect other people*

8. *Be willing to take action and make the changes real in your life*

As we become more observant and responsible for our thoughts, we will begin to notice things about ourselves that we have overlooked in the past. I remember a lovely lady from the Administration Department at the Victoria State Opera who would beam at me every time I came into rehearsals and ask me how I was feeling. She was sincerely interested in me and, although I always responded kindly,

I never stopped to talk with her or could ever remember her name. This in itself was puzzling, as I usually had an excellent memory for peoples' names, until one day I realised that I really didn't care what her name was as she held no influence in my life and could not further my career prospects. I was horrified to catch sight of myself making such a distinction of power and position, so the next time I saw her I made a point of learning her name and began to get to know her better. Why is it that I suddenly noticed my dismissive behaviour towards this woman and why had I never noticed it before? What was different about that day from any other, and why did I make the effort to change the way I was treating her? I can only surmise that my intuitive voice was speaking loudly, which forced me to tune in and listen. In doing this, my attitude changed, and when my attitude changed I felt much better about myself, which told me that this inner voice or feeling was the one I should look for and follow in the future.

"Intuition is a spiritual faculty that does not explain, but simply points the way."
- Florence Scovel Shinn

If you are still reading this book you are more than likely ready to access the deeper parts of yourself and to *start accessing your voice* from a place of clarity and empowerment. You may also be experiencing some form of conflict, where one part of you is excited about new possibilities but the other is feeling trepidation at the prospect of relinquishing a solely rational and cerebral approach to singing. Trusting in and acting upon the guidance of intuition is an art that requires ongoing discipline and commitment. The more we practice the more comfortable we will become with the inner voice of *knowing,* rather than the limited and fearful instructions of the conscious mind. Much is documented about how sound is conceived physically, but not much is said about the mental process vital to the flow of this sound once it is born. Singing is an internal experience, and an internal experience is felt from within, and whatever is felt from within cannot be adequately analysed or understood by anything but the intuitive mind. You are conceiving and birthing sound in every single moment that you are speaking or singing. You are tuning into language, pitch, rhythm, and emotions, coordinating them and sending them out into the world via an instrument that is inhabited by you. Physical? Yes. Mental? Yes. Intuitive? Absolutely.

What we resist persists
The more you focus on a problem, the more you empower it. Whether it is a thought, an emotion, or a situation, the fact of the matter is that we suffer only because we want things to be different. Most of the time it is not the experience itself that creates the suffering, but the *resistance* to it, coupled with an idealistic belief that it should have happened or be happening in some other way. I hear so many singers brutally complaining about their vocal flaws whilst conducting endless post mortem on less than sterling personal performances. Subsequently, more and more energy is invested into maintaining a running commentary on the inadequacies of themselves, with less and less emphasis placed on validation and the creating of what they want. Focusing on the things you do not like or want only continues to attract them. But by putting your attention on your gifts, your talents, and the things you want to achieve, you will find yourself moving in a very different direction.

Many a student has resisted this transition, but never anyone more so than Rick. Rick was 21 and a superb musician. Already an established pianist and musical director in Australia, he was now studying for a degree in musical theatre. A self-professed perfectionist, Rick had an inner critic like no other I had ever seen, and he would reprimand, criticise, and sneer at virtually every sound he uttered. Being such an accomplished pianist, he could not tolerate the fact that his voice was not exceptional, which only served to shut him down even more. Neither could he understand that - for him - the piano was so much easier to control because it was an external object, and that because his voice was inside of him, the way in which it was accessed and controlled was completely different. At times, the experience of being his own worst enemy was almost intolerable for him, and he would become locked with frustration when I pressed him to turn inward for the answers. He wanted me to explain the unexplainable in *literal* and *finite* terms, so my analogies were met with impatience, and my suggestions of intuitive imagery with a stony face or polite dismissal. Although I understood that his disgust was aimed at his own inadequacies, I was unsure of what else I could do without compromising my own integrity and began to dread the hours when I would have to humor or cajole him into the frame of mind where I knew his voice could flourish. "It takes so much energy to be positive and *alive!*" he complained one day. This was an arduous journey for us both, but mutual respect and the knowledge that we both had things to learn from this tenuous relationship prompted me to temper my usual course of action and realise that he needed to find his own answers in his own way and that this was not the time.

Pursuit of pleasure, avoidance of pain
Human behaviour is motivated by two things only - the *pursuit of pleasure* and the *avoidance of pain* - so whatever it is we decide gives us comfort is the direction we will take, and the things we deem uneasy or painful, we will try to avoid. Perversely, staying within our comfort zone is often not comfortable at all or conducive to growth and happiness but until it becomes a place of intolerable pain, we will not choose to do things any other way.

Sitting on the Fence
With every choice there will be a sacrifice, which is often why we make no choice at all, but the minute you become conscious of other alternatives, sooner or later you will have no option but to act upon them. Indecision or apathy will only exacerbate feelings of unworthiness and render you someone who endlessly complains about limitation but never does what is needed for lasting change to occur.

What you don't know won't hurt you
The truth of a statement relies on the context in which it is being used, but all too often it is taken as a blanket statement, leaving it unquestioned and underexplored. It is true that if you have not heard the vicious gossip someone has spread about you, you are certainly far better off for not having heard it, but if you are starving and no one tells you that there is food stored in a cupboard you have not yet discovered, they are denying you your life. What you do not know *can* and *does* hurt you, as the human spirit becomes agitated and restless when it is searching for itself. Therefore, it is imperative that we know where to turn for advice and what to do with it when it is given.

A work in progress
Your negative inner dialogue has taken years to develop, so converting it into one of power and affirmation will also take time. I have witnessed many a devastated singer exiting the stage unable to understand why the positive affirmations he or she had uttered minutes before a performance did not override or save him or her from the usual defeatist outcome. Placing a *band aid* on a deep wound will not stop it bleeding or prevent infection, so a much deeper palliative process is necessary if healing is to occur.

When we are inspired and excited about the idea of positive life changes, it is easy to become impatient and to try to bypass the gestation period necessary for all new life to grow. Despite the current belief that there is no time to spend on *mastery*, you do in fact have a lifetime to explore a more positive way of moving in the world. It is important to begin in small and gentle ways until you are feeling confident and strong, and only then should you begin to tackle the more ingrained issues of your subconscious.

Recently one of my students came into his lesson complaining of having difficulty performing the songs he had once found easy, due to the fact that he was trying to replace deeply ingrained vocal problems with all the things we had been working on in class. I commended him for being so willing to trust me, but explained that it was counter-productive for him to relinquish all that he knew in favor of the principles I was teaching him when they were still so foreign to him. I told him that even though he understood the concepts in his mind, he had not integrated them physically and, therefore, letting go of everything he had previously relied upon would leave his *house* empty. It takes time to inhabit new ways of thinking. Therefore, it is normal to feel a loss of control and security, but these feelings are only symptomatic of releasing outmoded behaviours and redundant belief systems. Once the process has begun it is pointless to resist, as a new identity is forming and you would not be allowing this to happen if your current ways were still serving you. You are a *work in progress* that is changing you for the better, and you need to trust in a process that will eventually allow you to break through to new forms of freedom and creativity.

In the initial stages of creating a more positive inner dialogue you will find your *critic* quite difficult to control, as its habitual reprimand will continue to trigger automatically until you are able to convert it into affirming statements. Although you cannot control when and where your negative voice will pipe up, you can control how you will respond to it, which immediately places you in a position of power irrespective of where you are in your development. Instead of agreeing with the negative voice, you can begin to ask yourself if the statements it is making are true. Repeating sentences to yourself like, "*I have a lovely voice, I auditioned so well today,* or *I know that I am talented enough to have a successful career*", will initially feel awkward and perhaps dishonest, but this is understandable as the comments you usually make to yourself have been largely negative. The more you say them, the easier it will become to hear them said about yourself and for you to actually begin to believe them. Focus on your accomplishments, your triumphs, and all the outstanding qualities others appreciate in you, and it will be impossible not to see the truth about yourself.

Exercises:

a) *Find a quiet place to sit or lie and begin to tune into your thoughts and feelings.*

b) *Listen to what the negative voice in your head is saying to you, and ask it why it is saying such things. Ask yourself if you deserve to be spoken to like that and if indeed you believe these statements to be true? If so, why?*

c) *Bring your thoughts to something you love to do and revel in the memory of whatever it is. Every time your negative voice wants to interrupt your joyful thoughts, ask it to stop being a wet blanket and promptly turn your thoughts back to the things you love.*

d) *Write down four or five statements you might use to encourage someone else, and then replace the word you with I.*

   Examples:

   - *Well done! You did an excellent job.*
     Well done! I did an excellent job.

   - *I know you can do it.*
     I know I can do it.

   - *You worked so hard for that opportunity. You really deserve it.*
     I worked so hard for that opportunity. I really deserve it.

   - *Wow, you are so inspirational!*
     Wow, I'm so inspirational!

e) *Repeat these sentences silently to yourself throughout the day, which will allow you to eventually turn them into automatic statements that will replace those that are counter-productive and negative.*

f) *Break a habit, follow a hunch or a random flash of inspiration, and see where it takes you, e.g., take a different to route to work from the one you normally travel, say hello to a stranger, go on a day trip without knowing where you are headed, or when someone you know pops into your head, call them to see how they are.*

g) *Begin reading books or articles that present new ideas and perspectives on spirituality, psychology and personal empowerment, and then find courses that can offer you personal experience of the principles you are reading about.*

NOTES:

14

RHYTHM AND RITUAL
Beating Your Own Drum

"He who trims himself to suit everyone will soon whittle himself away."

- Raymond Hull

Nothing in the world is permanent or fixed but it is important to be aware that whenever you move away from something, you will always be moving toward something else. Depending on what it is you are moving away from, the outcome will either be positive or negative. All forms of life, including the human body, respond rhythmically to the cycles of the sun, moon, and the seasons. These *biologic rhythms* take place during specific time cycles and are regulated by what we commonly know as our *body clock*. Although these rhythms can be reprogrammed through necessity or environmental influences, as with night shift workers who sleep during the day, they are genetically hard-wired into our cells, tissues, and organs, and if ignored, will eventually result in some form of physical or emotional dysfunction. The ever increasing demands and pressures of modern day living so often encourage or demand that we move away from, or work against, the natural inclination of our bodies. And in my opinion, the agitation and imbalance of the world today is a casualty of this. It is not always easy to pinpoint where imbalance begins, as decline is often gradual and accumulated over time. How often have you heard some one say, "How did I get here?" or "Where did my life go?" or "I didn't see it coming."

There is a well-known story about how a frog responds to a rapidly changing environment, which gives us valuable insight into how we find ourselves in non-conducive or uninhabitable places without suffering too much discomfort. When you place a frog in a saucepan of cold water and put it on the stove, it is quite happy to be there until the water begins to increase in temperature. Although the frog feels uncomfortable in the warmth, it is able to handle it and in a short while has adapted to the change. As the water becomes hotter, it feels more and more uncomfortable but still manages to acclimatise. Eventually, the frog boils to death as the water becomes too hot to survive and he is too weak to escape. On the other hand, if the frog had been thrown into boiling water, it would either have immediately jumped out or instantly died from shock. In a nutshell, if changing conditions are introduced slowly enough, we hardly notice the adverse effects until the situation is either chronic or irreversible.

No matter how tired my mother was she would always rise at 5am for what she called her *quiet time*. She would read, write, or simply potter around the house thinking her thoughts and doing whatever she needed to do to prepare for the day ahead. This *ritual,* she later told me, preserved her sanity throughout the seemingly endless years of family struggle, allowing her to continue *giving* to us all. Strangely, it appears I have adopted the same ritual for my own life and find myself agitated and ungrounded if I do not take this time before I start each day. I am the early to bed, early to rise type whose creative energy springs to life with the sunrise and hunkers down at night, which has often earned me the unsavory title of anti-social, reclusive, or conservative. And then there are those who seem to only connect with their creative juices in the wee hours of the morning when the world has gone to sleep. Many a time I have tried to go against my own flow in an effort to fit in socially, or to be a supportive partner to someone who has a diametrically opposed energy to mine, but this has never been sustainable and I quickly find myself moving back to the things that I find comfortable and *real*.

Warm baths, healthy food, nature, and simplicity are the things I seek when I'm distressed or in need of nurture, but these needs were not always easy to fulfill or so readily available. Such was the case when I relocated to Singapore, leaving Sydney's magnificent coastal views, ocean breezes, ravishing sunsets, and the wild and windy beaches that had been an integral part of my daily sustenance for seven years. I was excited to be starting a new phase of my life but nothing had prepared me for the culture shock I was to experience when I first arrived. Strangely, it was not the tropical heat that sent me into a tailspin, but rather the abrasive commercialism, endless construction, shopping mall madness, and the unfamiliar lack of personal space. It became clear to me that I needed to find a house that gave me the same kind of freedom and peace I had enjoyed in Australia. Miraculously I was *provided* with a magnificent Balinese-style house surrounded by trees and non-developed acreage, along with squirrels, monkeys, birds, butterflies, and even snakes. It has now been over seven years since my relocation but I continue to develop habits and rituals that allow me to thrive in a country that does not typically suit me.

Give or take?
To say that we must first *love* or *give to* ourselves before we can *love* or *give* to another is profound although rarely understood, as loving oneself means allowing yourself to have what makes you happy, which in turn allows you to share that happiness with others. The general consensus, however, is that a person who *gives* is more desirable than someone who *takes*, but the truth is that both have their extremes where neither one is balanced and only serves to stunt the development of the individual. To relinquish who and what you are in the name of giving to another renders you a victim and dulls the energy you would ordinarily be sharing, just as to take things only for yourself is to negate the reason you exist at all, which is to share and contribute constructively to others. Finding the balance, however, can be more than challenging.

Tara came into her singing lesson exhausted and in tears, and as emotional upheaval more often than not stores constriction in the throat, I needed to understand her distress before asking her to sing. Tara was popular, gregarious, and extremely empathetic, often going beyond the call of duty when supporting friends and colleagues. On this particular day, an ugly feud that had been festering for months between two of her female classmates had reached fever pitch. To her own detriment, she had been playing devil's advocate for weeks now by sympathetically lending an ear and offering possible solutions to the problem. But suddenly her good intentions were backfiring as her desire to remain neutral had become *unsatisfactory* to the girls and they were urging her to take sides. "I just want them to stop telling me every stupid detail," she sobbed. I asked her if she had told them this, and it was when she sadly shook her head, that I knew our spending an hour discussing the importance of *personal boundaries* was going to be far more constructive than practicing scales.

Boundaries
Boundaries make clear separations between the things we wish to keep for ourselves, and the things we are willing to share with others. If we do not create these dividing lines, it is easy to become embroiled in another's drama and end up living a life that is not our own. There are many reasons why we find ourselves the *victim* of another person's reality but, if observed intelligently, we will find a fascinating road map into our own personal patterns and insecurities. Each of us is conditioned to seek validation and approval, but validation and approval so often come from doing what other people want us to do. However, when doing what other people want us to do is not in alignment with

our own desires and needs, we will most certainly suffer some form of dissatisfaction or collapse. All her life Tara had been praised for her ability to take care of others and, despite craving her own space and solitude, was terrified that if she lived the way she wanted to she would no longer be loved and appreciated. The easiest way to convince a student to change a stressful situation is to help him or her face the harsh realities of continuing to live in that way. Stressful situations cannot be changed unless they are dealt with differently, and they cannot be dealt with differently unless the way in which they are perceived *changes*. I asked Tara to take some time to create clear boundaries based on what she needed and what she wanted for her life, and to then go and communicate this with her friends. The following week Tara literally bounded into her lesson well rested, happy, and re-energized after diplomatically telling the two bickering girls to "work it out themselves."

In Singapore there is a strong commitment to the *extended family* and it is not uncommon to find adults still living in the family home at the age of 35 and beyond. Few seem to have a healthy balance between living their own lives and filial responsibility and, in my experience, most are repressed by patriarchal dominance and hold no real expectation of an independent future.

Many of my local students face a dilemma when trying to practice at home due to sharing a bedroom with another sibling who needs to study, parents walking in and out of the room at will, or neighbours complaining that the sound of a practicing artist is intrusive and annoying. So in an attempt to remain respectful and considerate, my students will resort to suppressing and tempering their voices. This becomes immensely frustrating for me as I am teaching singers to let go of inhibition, but many of the cultural expectations are directly or indirectly fostering the opposite. Having come from a country with very different cultural sensibilities, I am often at a loss for constructive solutions other than to remind these students that it only takes a little initiative to change a situation for the better, if only in the smallest of ways.

Exercises:

a) *Ask yourself how you feel and what it is you need, e.g., "I feel stressed and overwhelmed and I need some time on my own."*

b) *Find at least one way to fulfil this need, e.g., go for a long walk, take a warm bath, lie down in a place with trees and running water, or simply have an early night.*

c) *Write down a list of things that you love to do and try to treat yourself to at least one of them every week.*

Where there's a will there's a way

Whenever I was on tour with a show, I always made it a priority to find a place where I could practice. It didn't matter to me if it was a hotel room, a friend's house, an abandoned classroom, or even a storeroom at the back of a theatre, as long as I could sing. I always found a place. When I was seventeen years old I worked as a clerk for a car insurance company in Melbourne, but after a mind-numbing year I swore that I would never work in an office again. I never did. I knew that

I could never relate to a knock on the door asking me to pipe down, or being an unwilling voyeur to intimate *love fests* and the high rise fallout of angry neighbouring tenants, so I chose never to live in a flat or an apartment. If you do not know what you feel, you cannot know what you need, and if you do not know what you need, your needs cannot be met. But it is in the *believing* that you *deserve* to have your needs met that it all comes apart. Why should self-worth or taking care of oneself begin and end with clean clothes, fresh makeup, and a tidy apartment? And why is it so hard to accept that our fundamental longing to be held, heard, and understood is just a deeper level of the same thing?

We are conditioned to believe that all *opportunity* lies in saying "yes" to things but, in fact, other opportunities arise when we say "no." For example, if I say "no" to dinner with friends, it opens up the opportunity for me to go home and spend an evening on my own; and if I say "no" to picking up a friend from the airport, I have the opportunity to make the deadline I have for my thesis without stress; and if I say "no" to a singing role that does not suit me, it opens an opportunity for me to accept a role that does. It is very important to understand that saying no to something does not have to be a judgement of the thing you are saying no to. It is merely a choice you are making based on what you feel and what you need at that particular time. This, of course, will take a great deal of practice as many will try to make you feel guilty about your apparent *selfish* behaviour, and you may well begin to undermine the validity of your decisions. However, it is imperative that you stay strong and follow what it is you truly feel.

Setting up boundaries, habits and routines

A. Time and Space - If you are constantly feeling rushed or pushed in your daily life, you do not have effective boundaries in place for yourself. Make a list of five things that you would like to have in your life and start making time and space for them. To do this, however, those five things must take priority over others less important to you. For example, my mother took *space* for herself every morning rather than sleeping in, knowing that this allowed her to face each day clearly and constructively. I like to arrive early for appointments to avoid the stress of being late, and close my doors to the world around 8pm in the evening rather than attending social gatherings or eating out. One of my friends loves to sit at the Botanic gardens with a fresh coffee and a newspaper *strategising* his latest business ventures, or playing pool and drinking single malt whisky with his closest male friends. Making space and setting time aside for the things we need or want to do allows us to fulfill our obligations and contribute to others more easily, so work out how much time you can set aside for these things and balance them against all your other responsibilities.

B. Habits and routines - There will always be reasons why you cannot make time and space for yourself, some of which will be valid but many that will not. If actions are to become habits they must be repeated regularly, which allows them to become part of your daily routine. The general consensus is that it takes thirty days to form a habit, so make that your starting point for the changes you wish to make to your life. If I were helping a singer create the necessary structure for vocal improvement I would suggest the following:

1. *Practice your singing daily at a specifically chosen time of the day. If this is not possible, do it sometime within that same day in the time that you have available.*

2. *Structure your practice into:*
   a) Warm up.
   b) Review and correct any technical issues from your last lesson.
   c) 'Sing in' the song you are currently working on with your teacher.
   d) Learn or research new repertoire.

C. Buffers - A buffer is something that *cushions* discordant or antagonistic energies and lessens the disturbance or irritation they may cause us. No matter how hard we may try, there will always be people and places that do not feel empowering to us. There are times when we should stay in a situation and persevere, but there are also times when things are simply incompatible.

Exercises:

a) *Notice the people and places that drain you and learn to diplomatically move away from them whenever and wherever you can.*

b) *Observe whether those who love you (e.g., family and friends) also regularly validate you. Spend the majority of your time with those who support, encourage, and inspire you and try to do the same for others around you.*

c) *Learn to say no to people and things when you are tired, ill, or anxious.*

d) *Spend time alone every day for planning, processing, regrouping and realigning yourself.*

The double-edged sword
There is always the danger that the things that set you free can also become your prison. Creating your own boundaries, routines, and rituals should never make you inflexible towards others or without spontaneity in your life. Be careful that your time spent alone does not become a self-imposed exile or a life of isolation, and make sure that your decision to avoid negativity and stressful environments does not turn into judgement and intolerance. Live in this world and enjoy it for all the wonderful things it can offer, but do not be bullied into living by another's values or agenda.

I have great admiration of those who do not conform. Not those who aggressively attack and rebel against the world, but those who flamboyantly *dance* their way through life, living truthfully and passionately. These people are often labeled eccentrics or misfits merely because they refuse to be limited by an already limited mindset, and yet they are so often of genius mind and profoundly reliable character. Others less obvious are simply comfortable in their own skin conducting their lives on their own terms and leading by example with integrity and wisdom.

You may wonder what filling a vase full of your favorite flowers, sending an inflammatory article to the local newspaper, sprinkling lavender on your bed sheets, or saying no to dinner with friends in favor of an evening alone has to do with singing well. But it is when you nurture your own happiness by allowing yourself to feel what you feel and do what you want to do, that your voice has the best possible chance of becoming confident and authentic.

We all have our own paths to travel and we all have our own particular life lessons to learn, but if I can inspire at least one *frog* to jump out of the *saucepan*, my job will be done.

NOTES:

15

THE HEAD TO THE HEART
The Longest Journey

"Efforts and courage are not enough without purpose and direction."

\- John F. Kennedy

Most things in life work in *duality* or *opposition.* Night/day, full/empty, up/down, and inside/outside are just some of the most basic examples where one not only *identifies* the other, but also *complements* and *completes* it. Neither can be called right or wrong, but too much time spent in either creates an imbalance or serious deficit in the other. Such is the reality with *thinking* and *feeling* and unless we remove ourselves from society and go and sit on a mountain, maintaining equilibrium and balance between them takes far more than a sharp mind and an optimistic heart.

Only part of our success in life can be attributed to intellectual achievements, as it is our emotional life that fuels our *aspirations* and *goals,* which ultimately reveal our true *purpose* for being in the world. A great deal of kudos is placed upon a person's I.Q. but not nearly enough importance is placed upon developing what is known as the E.Q. E.Q.is *heart* or *emotional intelligence,* which describes our capacity for *empathy, intuition, creativity, resilience, integrity, authenticity,* and *interpersonal* skills. Those who work from this place are the ones who tend to succeed creatively, not only fostering flourishing careers but also deep and lasting relationships. Moving away from limitation, judgement, and fear and into heart-centred purpose appears to take a lifetime to achieve, but nurture, kindness, empathy, and courage are, in fact, the most natural and fundamental traits of all human beings. Reclaiming *balance* and *control* of these areas is a challenging journey due to long-established patterns of behaviour and cultural conditioning, but those can be overridden if we learn to live from a place of *feeling* rather than *thinking.* It is never too late, or too soon for that matter, to begin the journey out of the *head* and back into the *heart* and, despite appearing daunting and somewhat illusive, it is the only place where true joy, creativity, and purpose will be found.

Although the action of singing is indeed a physical skill that can be coordinated mechanistically, authentic expression and communication can only come from the emotions. When the heart becomes involved in the action of singing, not only will the vocal result improve but you will also find that the *reason* you sing takes on a much higher *purpose* and *power*.

Power
It is difficult and somewhat awkward to see ourselves as "individuals of unlimited power and potential" when so much of the world has its focus on limitation and fear, but unless this perception changes it is not possible to live a life of creativity and fulfillment. One of the many wonderful stories Vikas Malkani told me when I attended his course *Shine* was of two boys standing at the edge of the ocean. One was holding a bucket and the other a cup. Both proceeded to scoop up the water from the ocean, but only the boy with the full bucket of water laughed joyfully and then continued on his way. The boy with the cup became angry and started shouting at the ocean. "Why did you give him a bucket of water and only give me a cup?" he cried. "My job is to fill whatever you bring to me and you only brought me a cup" said the ocean. "If you had asked me to give you a bucket full, I would have, and if you had asked for a truckload or even a lake full of water, I would have granted you that as well." Seeing that the boy did not understand, he continued to explain to him that as the ocean was infinite and unlimited, it could never become dry or empty and therefore no amount was too great. "The only limitation you have is your expectation for yourself," said the ocean, "and when you begin to ask for more, you will receive more."

Passion

People who love what they do have no difficulty working from the heart, as inspiration and celebration are glorious *byproducts* of doing the things we are passionate about. Many singers come from a place of weakness. No journey can be taken successfully if you are defeated before you begin, so it is important to understand that we all start with a small seed of *potential*. This potential may or may not be realised, but if you are realistic in your aspirations and goals there is no reason that the outcome will be anything less than successful. It is easy to fall into the trap of believing that success lies in notoriety or *high-profile* acclaim, but this is subjective and often short lived. On the other hand, working towards a life filled with the things you are passionate about will foster ongoing discovery and a sense of real achievement.

Presence

Once you are living the life you want for yourself, an interesting phenomenon begins to occur. Someone who may have once appeared ordinary and uninspiring now begins to exhibit an *inner light* or *presence,* which then starts to attract the attention of others. Suddenly doors begin to open and random opportunities begin to appear from the most unexpected places. When these doors do begin to open you must be ready to say "yes" and accept the gifts being offered by having a clear and practical *plan* of how you wish to move forward with your goals.

Plan

Passion and presence are not enough on their own, as a *plan of action* is the only thing that will convert *potential* into *tangible reality*. You must have a goal in mind so you can be clear about what kind of plan of action it is you need to take. For example, I wanted to be a soloist in an opera company so I firstly needed to do the training to become a proficient opera singer. I then had to audition well enough to be accepted into a company. When I was accepted as a chorus member, I gave myself the next five years to become good enough to be a leading lady. I did this by continuing my studies and setting myself apart from other chorus members by taking on extra unpaid work and scouting any suitable understudy roles. I was soon offered small parts, and within four years I was finally given my first break as a soloist.

To create an effective plan of action you need to ask yourself a few basic questions, and when you have clear and concise answers to them, you will be far more able to commit to the process necessary to achieve them:

1. *What is it you want to do?*

2. *Why do you want to do it?*

3. *When do you plan to have it done by?*

4. *How will you achieve your goals?*

So many levels and layers support the action of singing and, although each of them is important in their own right, they are only a part of the entire process and must learn to cooperate with each other. Only you, the singer, can know which of these areas needs the most attention, but this may change and vary as you travel the stages of vocal integration, and it will take ongoing diligence and discernment if you are to continue growing and developing as an artist.

Pedagogy

Vocal pedagogy covers all areas of singing, which include not only the physiological process of vocal production but also technique, artistic interpretation, and knowledge of the differences among musical styles and genres.

Practice

If you hope to master the intricacies and subtleties of vocal technique, it will demand daily practice. Mastering a skill requires experience, which takes time to acquire, and this asks a singer for *persistence* and *patience*. These qualities are not easy to sustain unless you have a deep sense of the *purpose* you have for doing it in the first place.

Peaks and Plateaus

Even with a deep sense of purpose, there will be continual challenges along the way. Reaching a *peak* or a *turning point* in your ability and/or career is exhilarating and rewarding to say the least, but inevitably there will be troughs and plateaus to deal with along the way. *Progress* comes in fits and spurts and just because changes are not always evident does not mean that they are not happening. Slow and steady progress leads to dramatic breakthroughs and when this happens, even more time will be needed to integrate the shifts before you will be ready to meet the next stage of your development. Allowing yourself to move at your own pace demands not only wisdom, but also a sense of humor and an ability to *play*.

Play

Keeping a healthy attitude towards your achievements and failures will be so much easier if you have a sense of humor and the ability to *play*. Without these, the process becomes intimidating and stressful. Today, the pressure of deadlines, fear of failure, and the unfortunate belief that laughter is a sure sign that you are not taking something seriously leave us crying more than we laugh and working so much more than we play. Learning to laugh in the face of adversity takes a certain kind of detachment from outcomes and an unshakable faith in yourself and your capabilities. This is only ever found when you put your goals and dreams into *perspective*.

Perspective

Although singing is indeed a powerful and miraculous gift it does not feed the hungry, bring a loved one back from the dead, prevent a terrorist action, or restore sight to the blind and therefore needs to be seen for *what it is* and *what it isn't*. The self-absorbed outpouring of grief at the failure to score a leading role in a show or at the inability to win over the masses to remain in a reality competition, becomes an absurd indulgence when compared to the troubles of the sick, the needy, and the handicapped. When you finally gain perspective in this area, personal imperfections and the inevitable insecurity that comes along with performing will become possible to handle and an expected part of the journey. Taking personal responsibility for your thoughts, feelings, and actions will also see you becoming self-aware and deciding to use your talents to give rather than to receive. This, in itself, adds volumes to your own personal *X factor* by replacing self-consciousness with *integrity* and *authenticity*. Perspective will come in time but not without deep contemplation. This you will find wherever there is *solitude* and *peace*.

Peace
Some of us choose to live simply, in quiet surroundings, that imbue harmony and healing, but most live and work in crowded cities among nonstop stimulus and abrasive vibrations. Many love the energy and excitement of these places but in a world that is becoming increasingly externally fixated, tranquil environments are far more difficult to find. It is now the *norm* to be hooked up to some computerised gadget or phone 24/7, and extraneous noise has become the global security blanket. Interpersonal relationships and intimacy are generally being delivered via text messages, emails, Facebook, and Twitter, and these are major contributors to communication breakdown and a growing sense of hopelessness and isolation. Language, poetry, art, and music are all casualties of this rapidly changing climate and, sadly, what is being overlooked is the insidious way in which these modern-day conveniences are undermining the way we use our voices.

> **"In the silence lie the subtleties and in the subtleties lie the answers."**
> *- A. Colliver*

Silence can be extremely confronting if you are not used to facing your feelings and emotions as, whenever there is minimal external stimulus, all the neglected and wounded parts of you will demand to be *heard* and *held*. Suddenly, all your fears and longings rise to the surface - and you will not necessarily like the way they look or feel. Many will bury them again with excuses and denial only to have to face them again somewhere down the line, but those who can acknowledge and embrace their dysfunction have taken the first steps towards expressing themselves from the *heart*. The only way you will ever trust your own instincts is if you stop asking other peoples' advice and allow your intuition its own voice. However, even if you are equipped with the right answers, you may not be ready to act upon them. This doesn't matter as long as you know that it is *you* who is making the decision *not* to act. This kind of *heart intelligence* is the very thing that allows us to use our voices with confidence and conviction.

Process
If you are someone who incessantly asks how long it will take to *arrive* at your destination, you are probably not motivated by a passionate desire to sing or someone who has a great interest in taking a journey of deep discovery. Incidentally, the answer to the question of how long it will take to arrive is probably "Never," as there are always other levels of awareness and expertise to achieve, but in time all who persevere will most certainly come to a place of technical reliability and vocal authenticity. Does it really matter if it takes a lifetime to achieve your dreams when you love what it is you are doing, and can it ever be called a waste of time if you are joyful and happy? Is it really true that all doors close when you reach a certain age, or do the priorities and strategies around your

goals and dreams simply need to change? I am now what is commonly referred to as a middle-aged woman, although I cannot begin to feel that this is *who* I truly am. It is an interesting voyage to find that maturity and confidence do indeed develop with age and experience, but how comforting it has been to realise that the child I once was still walks beside me laughing and chattering about who and what she wants to be when she grows up. Although it is true that certain options are no longer available, so many others of a much greater interest and importance *are*. Hindsight is a marvelous equalizer in the way it allows us to look back at all the twists and turns and highs and lows in our lives, only to see that they were, in fact, perfect lessons for where we were at that particular time. Suddenly, the investment we have in past grievances and failures begins to pale in comparison to a present moment that promises a new perspective and a new beginning.

On a recent walk I passed an old lady shuffling along the street in what appeared to be a valiant attempt to jog, her tired face and sad eyes sitting wearily atop her hunched shoulders and stubborn body. But when I looked downwards, what I saw prompted a tangible shift within me: her feet were *entombed* in a stunning pair of indescribably vibrant and optimistic red running shoes that were obviously ready and raring to go. How incongruous they were with where this woman appeared to be in her life, but how apt those red shoes are for the dream she apparently holds for herself. Never before have I been so clearly reminded that who we truly are is never far below the surface, and that all creativity will find a way to express itself one way or another.

Conclusion

"The desire to sing is the pull to return to who you truly are."
– A. Colliver

Think back to the times you have seen a baby taking its first steps. Joyful encouragement abounds and no one dares to push for more, lest the child should become discouraged and simply decide that it is not safe to try to walk again. No matter how old we are, we will all be taking *baby steps* in some area of our lives and must be allowed to fall and feel safe enough to get up and try again. We are living in interesting times where superficialities reign and the undertow of negativity is strong, so you will have to work hard to maintain creative equilibrium and trust in your talents and in your path. Life is not an accident and we are not here without purpose or power, so each one of us needs to decide who we wish to be and take action to make it a reality. Music nourishes and heals and has the power to transcend separation and although, for some, singing has been a cultural expression for centuries, for others it is still an empty space waiting to be filled. Pure and unadulterated potential, your voice waits to be invited to the party of your imagination, happy to rise and fall with your sorrow and joy, or randomly laugh and play for no reason at all. Your voice will expose you and leave you naked and unsure, but in that vulnerability you will find a kind of freedom unlike any other experience. To fear your voice is to fear yourself and that simply cannot be justified. Today is a new day with new challenges and new difficulties, but also with limitless opportunities to change the way you look at yourself, and others. Now is the time to acknowledge what it is you feel and what it is you need in your life to truly flourish and thrive. Despite the messages much of the world is sending us today, happiness is your birthright and fulfilling the needs of your deepest creative potential is your only responsibility. There are no exceptions…and yes, dear traveler, anybody can sing.

The End

ACKNOWLEDGEMENTS

My deepest love and gratitude to Brian and Joy Colliver for my education and ethics, my brothers and sisters for our childhood memories, and my *soul sister* Rosalie, for continuing to enhance my life with her sweetness and generosity. Deb Thurley for inspiring me to write *Child's Play* and *Rhythm and Ritual*, John (Johnny) Sharpley for keeping me politically correct and reminding me that not everybody has an Australian sense of humour, and Juan Jackson for *watching my back* every step of the way.

To all my courageous *case studies*, thank you for allowing me to use your names and share your stories with the world. Your struggles and triumphs will serve as an inspirational bridge to all who come after you.

To Ferdi Trihadi for his brilliantly original illustrations, Joan Melton for her immense knowledge, integrity, and speedy editing, Crispian Chan for his innovative ideas for the book layout, Tim Garner for his wordsmith's flair and skilled proofreading, Debbie Phyland, Kit Chan, John Robertson, Chris Nolan, Deb Thurley, John Sharpley, Ellis Jones, and Michael Corbidge for their humbling endorsements of this labour of love.

To my much loved colleagues Shaun Murphy, Tony McGill, Chloe Dallimore, Andrew Ross, Tony Knight, Vanessa Fallon Rohanna, Tanee Poonsuwan and Adrian & Tracie Pang for their generous testimonials.

To my vocal teachers, Elinor Morcom, Gary May, Greg Urisich, and Michael Parker, and to Seth Riggs and Jo Estill for their vocal research and methodology.

To my spiritual mentors Deepak Chopra, Marianne Williamson, Og Mandino, Wayne Dyer, Neale Donald Walsh, and Byron Katie for their inspirational books throughout my life and to Brendan Burchard, Christian Pankhurst, Rachael Jayne Groover, and Vikas Malkani for their life changing courses.

And most of all, to my best friend Jai, for showing me the true meaning of unconditional love.

Illustrator - Ferdi Trihadi (www.ferditrihadi.com)

Editor - Joan Melton (joan.melton@joanmelton.com)

Setting & Layout - Crispian Chan

Proofreading - Tim Garner (www.timgarnerproductions.com)

Photography - Juan Jackson

Printing - Tien Wah Press (Pte) Limited

Publisher - PaperKite Studios (www.paperkitestudios.com)

Brendan Burchard - *www.brendanburchard.com*

Christian Pankhurst - *www.christianpankhurst.com*

Rachael Jayne Groover - *info@theyinproject.com*

Vikas Malkani - SoulCentre - *www.soulcentre.org*

THOSE WHO WISH TO SING WILL ALWAYS FIND A SONG

Amanda Colliver began her career as a singer/songwriter, actress and recording artist, going on to enjoy a successful 23 year career as a soloist with all the major Opera Companies and Symphony Orchestras in Australia. Recognised as a passionate and innovative educator, she is one of the few to blur the boundaries between classical and contemporary singing. Students such as Hugh Jackman, Nicole Kidman and Ewan McGregor are just a few of the famous names to frequent her private singing practice, making her one of the most sought after and respected teachers in the industry today. *Can Anybody Sing?* is a powerful testimonial to decades of research into the physical, mental and psychological barriers that prevent one and all claiming their true and authentic voice. Amanda is currently developing *The Colliver Method*, and continues to mentor singers through workshops, master-classes, and private tuition.

"Amanda is more of a Guru than a vocal coach and has not created a technical manual on how to sing, but rather takes an extremely philosophical and holistic viewpoint towards the art of singing. If you are a seasoned singer you will most definitely experience a breakthrough. If you are a beginner, there is no better way to set yourself straight from the start. Lucky you!"
KIT CHAN - Singer, Actress, Producer, Creative Director.

"Some teachers are good, others are inspirational. One of the most diverse and talented artists I have ever worked with."
TONY MCGILL, Musical Director, Arranger, Performer, Program Director, LASALLE College of the Arts

"This new book is truly one of a kind! From the perspective of a remarkable teacher and performer, Colliver provides unique insight into the life and training process of professional singers across a range of genres. A fascinating and inspiring work for anyone who sings or wants to sing."
JOAN MELTON, PhD, ADVS Writer, Researcher, Voice Coach, NYC

"Very simply, Amanda Colliver is the best in the business!"
ADRIAN & TRACIE PANG, Artistic Directors of Pangdemonium Productions

"Amanda's book is a rare blend of wisdom and practical exercises drawing on her vast experience as a performer, teacher, and mentor. Her writing lays bare all the layers of misconception and half-baked theories that you and I might have about how to sing. "Can Anybody Sing?" is a road map and action plan that shows us how to fall in love with our voices, ourselves, and our lives."
DEBORAH THURLEY - Mum, businesswoman, meditation and yoga teacher.

ISBN 978-1-4836-3768-6

Xlibris

PaperKite Studios
www.paperkitestudios.com

CPSIA information can be obtained
at www.ICGtesting.com
Printed in the USA
LVIC07n1517180813
348456LV00009B